The Scholastic Debater

The Scholastic Debater

Dr. Nicholas M. Cripe
Butler University

Dr. Royce E. Flood
Butler University

Alistair Press
A Division of The Educational Video Group
Greenwood, Indiana

CONTENTS

PREFACE

It has been nearly a decade since we published *Modern Competitive Debate*, that alone would seem sufficient reason for a new revised edition. Even more compelling, however, is the fact that the 1980's was a decade of unparalleled change in the practice of academic debate. Many of these alterations have rendered obsolete some of the discussions and advice offered in this text; and, therefore, out of a concern for the students and coaches using this book we felt compelled to offer this revision.

Our original intent was to incorporate the new theory and practice into the existing chapters, particularly those on debating the affirmative and the negative. A brief attempt to do so revealed to us the futility of such an approach. We quickly realized how confusing such a description would be, especially to the beginners who comprise a large part of our audience. As a result, we have merely reworked the existing chapters and have placed the discussion of the new techniques in a separate, thirteenth chapter. This will allow the beginning student to master the traditional approaches to the activity and then to understand current practice by means of comparison with the original nature of debate. In addition, this allows those coaches to whom recent developments are anathemas to ignore the final chapter.

As was our hope with the original edition of this volume, we trust that new generations of students and coaches will profit from what we have learned over years of participation in this activity— which we still believe can be one of the most enjoyable and beneficial the academic world has to offer its students.

REF & NMC

1
CHAPTER

Introduction

Why should you debate? Why should academic institutions sponsor debate programs? Dr. Ernest Fremont Tittle gave the most satisfactory answer in a commencement address at Northwestern University many years ago when he said, "The voice of the ordinary man may not carry very far. All the more reason, as far as it does carry, it should be made as clear and compelling as possible." In our society, citizens who cannot express their ideas with the spoken and written word in a clear fashion are voiceless citizens, people whose ideas will never be heard; and for some twenty-five hundred years educators have found that one of the best methods for teaching students how to think and to express those thoughts in a clear and compelling manner has been through training in debate.

The History of Debate

The "Father of Debate" was probably Protagoras of Abdera (481-411 B.C.) who is believed to have been the first to teach argumentation by organizing contests among his pupils.[1] The Greek and Roman philosophers also employed this method, and in the medieval universities part of the curriculum frequently prescribed Latin syllogistic disputation. Harvard and Yale introduced this form of training in the seventeenth century, but it was not popular with the students.[2] In the early eighteenth century, Harvard students debated in English in their clubs, and by the middle of the century Yale required courses in forensics.

In the late 1700's and early 1800's literary societies dedicated to debating, such as Phi Beta Kappa (1776), sprang up on the campuses of many colleges. As higher education moved west to Ohio, Indiana, and Illinois, so did the literary societies and debate. The first intercollegiate debate apparently took place on November 29, 1872, in Evanston, Illinois, between the Adelphic Society of Northwestern University and the Athenaeum Society of Chicago University.[3] The first intercollegiate debate for a decision was held on May 5, 1881, between the Phi Alpha Society of the University of Illinois and the Adelphi Society of Knox College.[4] Intercollegiate debating did not become popular, however, until Harvard and Yale met in two debates in 1892. Interest in debate at Harvard had been created because undergraduates had debated in their prep schools where interscholastic competition had commenced in 1887. With Harvard and Yale putting their stamp of approval on competitive debating, the activity was "in."[5] By 1900 intercollegiate debate was a permanent activity on many campuses, and the debate teams were meeting two and three opposing schools a year.

During the depression period of the 1930's, audience debating rapidly declined when tournament debating began to flourish as a way to finance more competition for less cost. The founding of the National Forensic League in 1924 provided high school debaters with the opportunity for national competition. Following World War II and the inauguration of the National Debate Tournament at the United States Military Academy in 1947, tournament debating became the prevalent form of the activity on both the college and high school levels.

For the next twenty years, not only was tournament debating literally the only type practiced, but an agreed-upon national topic was the only proposition employed. Since the 1970's, however, "off-topic" debate has been increasing on the college level. The Cross-Examination Debate Association, which advocates non-national topic debates, has been growing steadily. Delta Sigma Rho— Tau Kappa

Alpha and Pi Kappa Delta both employ "off-topic" formats at their national conferences. "Off-topic" debating on the high school level has increased greatly with the growing popularity of the Lincoln-Douglas format.

There has also been a marked increase in audience debates in which the two schools participating agree upon a topic, who will uphold which side, the format, and the time and place, just as did schools in the old days before tournament debating. The big difference now is that there is usually an audience decision rather than one by a panel of lawyers and/or court judges.

Thus, while most debating is still done on a national topic at a tournament, more and more debating is being practiced "off-topic" either at tournaments or before audiences. Academic debate offers diversified opportunities to its participants, both on the high school and college level.

Values of Debate

Debate's long life as an academic activity does not necessarily answer the question asked at the beginning of this chapter: why debate? A major reason is that being an active participant in a debate program provides a uniquely enriching experience for the participant that you will seldom find in any other scholastic activity. For students who enjoy keen competition, who enjoy using their minds, and who enjoy receiving recognition for achievement, debate can be a most pleasurable and valuable activity. Programs subscribing to the ideals expressed by Dr. Stanley Rives— and many do— can be of real value to the participating students. According to Dr. Rives, the emphasis of such a program "should be upon thorough research and analysis and advancement of reasoning and evidence in support of positions on public questions that are communicated effectively to a variety of audiences."[6]

A program striving to achieve the above goals is probably as valuable an experience as a student can find in a school no matter what that student's intended profession. Most of us can come up with a good rejoinder to an argument, given an hour or two. In debate the proper rejoinder must be generated almost immediately in a situation that has the speaker under pressure. Inherent in debate is the almost spontaneous attack and defense of the reasoning and evidence used in developing arguments. Debaters who are properly taught learn to recognize valid reasoning and to handle fallacious argument; they learn the value of supporting positions with evidence that will stand close scrutiny and immediate attack; they learn to organize and present those arguments clearly. They also learn that decisions are made in the minds of the listeners and that they must operate within the confines of a very limited time schedule. Debate forces its participants to think, organize, and present, and to do all of them quickly and clearly.

In addition debaters gain something equally valuable from their debate experience—good work habits. You cannot maintain the excellent grades expected of a debater; do the research, preparation, and practice demanded by debate; give up numerous weekends for travel and debating; plus spend the time demanded for audience debates and not develop good work habits. You will learn to manage your time.

To best achieve the values offered by debating, the debate program should be both tournament and audience oriented to assure the opportunity of learning to communicate "effectively to a variety of audiences." Tournament debaters soon learn that analysis, research, and practice can cut down on losses and increase victories. Losing is not an enjoyable experience. However, debaters who participate in tournament debating only may experience difficulty learning how to speak to a non-specialist "real life" audience— the type of listeners with whom audience debaters are dealing. These same debaters, given the added experience of live audience debates, soon realize the importance of skillfully presenting what they say.

Audience debate does provide participants with a more "real life" experience (gaining a desired response from a group of people) than does debating before a single judge for a decision based mainly on theories of argumentation as interpreted by that particular judge. Unfortunately, audience debating, with its needed emphasis on delivery skills and interesting presentational techniques, can fail to impose the intellectual rigor demanded of tournament debate. Tournament debating, based as it is on winning decisions with analytical, refutative, and research skills, hones these various abilities for the participant in a way that seldom seems to be achieved by the non-competitive audience programs.

No other academic program can teach you so many valuable skills as effectively and quickly as can a well conducted debate program which, if at all possible, will give you the opportunity to participate in both tournament and audience debates where delivery is not neglected in tournament rounds nor are analysis and reasoning slighted in the audience presentations.

Not only does such a program give you training in developing the skills already mentioned, it also provides you a learning opportunity sorely needed for citizenship in a democratic society based upon freedom of speech and the exchange and testing of ideas. The school-sponsored debate program emphasizes, in a manner not possible in the regular classroom, a code of ethics aimed at preserving the right to speak out in public. "Democratic society cannot exist without free discussion," observed Sidney Hook in his essay, "The Ethics of Controversy."[7] Stanley Rives, in his article on "Ethical Argumentation," adds:

> The existence of a free and orderly society dedicated to human happiness and welfare requires ethical conduct of its members. Our belief that argumentation and debate play an important role in the functioning and preservation of our free and democratic society requires not only that we promote an understanding of the methodology of debate, but also that we develop the practice of ethical argumentation.[8]

While debate holds no monopoly on teaching ethics and freedom of speech, a properly conducted debate program does emphasize the practice of ethical argumentation. Ethical debating is solely dependent on the individual debaters, debate coaches, and judges. The basic responsibility for such a program lies with the forensics teacher; this person must make it quite clear that unethical practices will not be tolerated in the program. Dedication to ethical standards is an individual decision, but the basis for those standards is inherent in the purpose of debate. Stripped to its most essential purpose, debate is the search for the best solution to a controversial problem and the communication of that solution by means of argumentation. A code of **ethics** for debate cannot merely be reduced to a list of do and don't commandments; it is simply a dedication to intellectual honesty and excellence.

The simplicity of the code should not deceive you, however, for those who seek the best assume many responsibilities. The debater has an ethical responsibility to research the proposition as thoroughly as possible, thus learning all that can reasonably be expected to be known about the topic. A rigorous analysis of the proposition should reveal all the issues and arguments inherent in the topic.

Having thoroughly researched and analyzed the proposition, the ethical debater then faces the responsibility of using sound facts and expert opinions to support rational arguments. This means the debater must have a strong working knowledge of the tests of evidence and of the various modes of reasoning. It means that the arguments must now be organized and presented in a manner that does not distort the reasoning or the evidence or deceive the opposition or the audience. At the same time, however, it means that the strongest case possible has been presented, either for or against the proposition.

Debate, to be done well, demands a great deal from the director of the program and from the participants. There is no easy way to conduct or to participate in an ethical debate program. The value stemming from the sacrifice of time and energy is the acquisition of the skills and ethics of a successful debater. These skills will remain with the student long after academic debate days are just pleasant memories.

NOTES

1. Bromley Smith, "The Father of Debate: Protagoras of Abdera," *Quarterly Journal of Speech,* IV (March, 1918), pp. 196-215.
2. David Potter, ed., *Argumentation and Debate, Principles and Practices* (New York: The Dryden Press, 1954), p. 6.
3. Otto F. Bauer, "The Harvard—Yale Myth," *The AFA Register,* XI (1963), p. 20.
4. Potter, p. 12.
5. Potter, pp. 13-14.
6. James H. McBath, ed., *Forensics as Communication: The Argumentative Perspective* (Skokie: National Textbook Company, 1975), p. 96.
7. Jerry M. Anderson and Paul J. Dovre, eds., *Readings in Argumentation* (Boston: Allyn and Bacon, 1968), p. 6.
8. Stanley Rives, "Ethical Argumentation," *Journal of the American Forensic Association,* I, No. 3 (Sept., 1964), p. 79.

2
CHAPTER

The Basics of Debate

Whenever you engage in a competitive activity, you must have a thorough understanding of the rules of the game. One of the first questions raised about a new activity is "how is it played?" or "what are the rules?" Thus in football a defensive back learns it is illegal to tackle a receiver before the ball arrives; a sprinter on a track team discovers that a false start may result in disqualification.

The competitive activity called debate also has numerous rules connected with it and, as with other contests, these rules serve two basic functions. First, they prescribe a definite set of actions and conditions, so that each participant may know what can and cannot be done. Secondly, the rules create play balance so that neither side has an undue advantage over the other due to the structure of the contest. The rules described in this chapter relate specifically to academic debate, but may, with a few alterations, be adapted to other forms of the activity as well.

The Structure of Debate

An academic debate takes place between two teams, usually of two persons each and is centered around a **proposition**, frequently a **proposition of policy**, which calls for a change from the way things are done at present (see Chapter 3). One side, known as the **affirmative**, is assigned to defend this proposition and thus to advocate a change in action; the other side, known as the **negative**, attacks the proposition. The organization of most academic debates follows this pattern:

1st affirmative constructive (1AC)
affirmative cross-examined by negative
1st negative constructive (1NC)
negative cross-examined by affirmative
2nd affirmative constructive (2AC)
affirmative cross-examined by negative
2nd negative constructive (2NC)
negative cross-examined by affirmative
1st negative rebuttal (1NR)
1st affirmative rebuttal (1AR)

2nd negative rebuttal (2NR)
2nd affirmative rebuttal (2AR)

Thus, the affirmative, which has to prove the desirability of change, both opens and closes the contest. The negative, in order that both sides may have equal speaking time, benefits from a long block in the middle of the debate. This is very similar to courtroom procedure where the prosecution (the affirmative) tries to alter the existing situation (the assumption of innocence on the part of the defendant) and thus has both the first and the last word.

While there is considerable flexibility in what each speaker may do, over the years debate has become somewhat stylized and each speech has taken on certain specific responsibilities. Generally, the first affirmative has the duty of delivering the entire affirmative constructive presentation. In the typical policy debate this consists of two parts: the **case** (which is the reason for change) and the **plan** (which is the specific change being offered). The first negative speaker usually concentrates on the case, trying to prove that change is unnecessary. The second affirmative replies to the first negative, attempting to restore and advance the case position. The second negative shifts the focus of the debate and attacks the plan, trying to show that it is undesirable. During these four constructive speeches, all original material must be introduced—the rebuttals are for presenting new evidence or extending arguments. No brand new arguments are allowed in the rebuttals.

The first negative rebuttalist returns to the case and responds to the second affirmative constructive. The first affirmative rebuttal, often considered the most difficult speech in the debate, attempts to deal with the previous two negative speeches, addressing first the plan arguments, since those have not yet been attacked, and then returning to the case. The final two rebuttal speakers deal with as much material as possible on both case and plan and attempt to summarize the debate from their team's perspective. It should be noted at this point that as a result of fundamental changes in the nature of debate on the college level in the 1980's, these traditional speaker responsibilities have been considerably altered. This new approach will be thoroughly discussed in Chapter 13. Chapter 3, in the section on stock issues, will help clarify the different duties of first and second affirmative speakers in propositions of judgment.

Each of the speeches has a set time limit. In high school most debates have eight-minute constructives, three-minute cross-examination periods, and four-minute rebuttals. For collegians the cross-examination remains three minutes long, but the constructives and rebuttals are lengthened to ten and five minutes respectively. In most debates timekeepers indicate the time remaining to the speakers by use of printed cards. Debaters are expected to be ready to speak very soon after their opponents have finished. In some high school contests practically no intervening time is allowed. In most college debates, each team is allowed ten minutes of preparation time during the debate, to be divided up as the speakers wish.

Key Concepts

In addition to the general rules, there are four concepts which must be clearly understood by all debaters. The first of these is **presumption**. Presumption may be defined as a bias in favor of existing institutions or ways of acting, sufficient to keep things as they are until good reason for change is shown. Current structures or actions are usually referred to as the **present system** or the *status quo*. In a debate, presumption rests with the negative as long as they defend the present system. The affirmative may never gain presumption, although the negative, by abandoning the present system, can lose it.

There are three major reasons for the existence of presumption. The first is that it helps to give order and stability to the universe. Mankind is essentially a conservative animal, preferring rational and orderly behavior to whim, chance, or caprice. If we did not presume in favor of what is, then advocates of change would have no responsibility to show that their changes would be beneficial or even needed. Thus we would constantly be changing, and matters would be in such a state of flux that no one would know what to expect of the world from day to day. To use a very simple example, imagine what confusion would result if the meaning of traffic light colors were to change randomly from day to day. By giving a built-in advantage to what presently exists, we prevent haphazard or useless change.

Secondly, presumption provides a hedge against the unknown dangers or risks which are inherent in any change. We are generally familiar with what currently exists; we have seen it in operation and we know what is good and what is bad about it. No one, however, can read the future; and no matter how thoroughly a proposal has been studied, there are still unknowns in it simply because it has never been tried. Thus, any time we change we risk unseen disasters. It was this idea which Shakespeare was expressing when he had Hamlet remark in his famous soliloquy:

> to die; – to sleep: –
> To sleep! perchance to dream: – ay, there's the rub;
> For in that sleep of death what dreams may come,
> When we have shuffled off this mortal coil,
> Must give us pause.

By presuming in favor of the *status quo* and thus requiring advocates of change to prove the strong desirability of their proposal, we assure that even if unknown disaster occurs, enough advantage has been gained to offset it.

Finally, as a practical matter, presumption provides the basis for breaking a tie in debate. As with a basketball or baseball game, a debate is not allowed to end in a tie. Presumption allows the debate judge to cast his ballot—for the negative, of course— even when all the issues appear deadlocked.

Over the last decade or so, two schools of thought and practice have arisen within the debate community which are at variance with this traditional view of presumption. The first of these is an interesting philosophical position, which commands the allegiance of but a small minority of collegiate coaches and debaters. The second is rapidly becoming the dominant view on the college level and has made major inroads into the high schools as well.

The first view is generally labelled **hypothesis testing**. The believers in this system argue that presumption rests not with the present system, but against the proposition. Thus, a negative may abandon the status quo and still retain presumption. It is usually not wise to argue such a position unless one is certain that the judge is a believer in the hypothesis testing approach.

The second view may be referred to as **policy systems comparison**. This quite complex set of beliefs and practices, which is the subject of Chapter 13, essentially abandons the entire concept of presumption. It will be the responsibility of the debater, after mastering both the traditional and modern systems, to utilize in a given debate that which best meets the beliefs and prejudices of the judge.

A second important term, and one closely linked with presumption, is **burden of proof**. Burden of proof is the responsibility of the affirmative to present a case strong enough to overcome presumption and thus create acceptance of the proposition. If there were no negative present and the affirmative presented a case of such strength that the judge, after hearing it, was willing to change, the burden of proof would have been fulfilled. This burden always rests with the affirmative; it never shifts, and the affirmative cannot escape it.

The third significant term is **burden of rebuttal**, sometimes known as the **burden of rejoinder** or the **burden of going forward**. This duty, which rests alternately with each team, is the responsibility to continue the debate until the time or speech limits have been met. Immediately after the first affirmative speech, this duty rests with the negative; after the first negative constructive it reverts to the affirmative, and so forth. If for some reason one team refused to exercise this duty (that is, refused to speak when it became their turn), the debate would naturally fall to the other side.

Finally, there is the term *prima facie*. This often misunderstood concept refers to the requirement on the affirmative to present a full, complete case which contains all the elements necessary to establish the desirability of change. Liberally translated from Latin the phrase means "on first being constructed." This implies a duty to fully establish the case before asking the judge to accept it. Some have interpreted this to mean that the entire affirmative case must be presented in the first constructive. While such presentation may be a good idea, it is too narrow to insist upon it as an absolute requirement. After all, there are two constructive speeches during which original material may be presented, and it would seem unnecessarily restricting to require that the affirmative can add nothing new after their initial speech. Affirmatives must realize, however, that they cannot legitimately ask for acceptance of their case until they have fulfilled all the burdens incumbent upon them; that is, until they have presented a *prima facie* case.

With an understanding of the basic structure of academic debate and with a thorough knowledge of the key concepts of the activity, you are now ready to analyze the proposition.

3
CHAPTER

Analysis of the Proposition

A debate occurs because someone is advocating a solution to a controversial problem and someone else refuses to accept that solution. If there is to be any hope for a satisfactory conclusion to the debate, certain definite procedures must be followed by all involved.

Framing the Proposition

First, the participants must make certain that they are all debating the same problem. This is accomplished by having the debate centered around a precise statement called a **proposition**. Formally defined, a proposition is a declarative sentence which expresses a judgment that the audience is asked to accept or reject. In the real world, advocates often find they have to spend considerable time carefully **framing** the proposition before they can successfully employ the argumentative process; in academic debate a committee of experts words the topic for the competitors.

Once the proposition has been worded, it must be classified. There are two major types of propositions: judgment and policy.[1] The first, which is more commonly used in audience debate situations, asks that a decision be made concerning the truth or worth of a statement. Thus, "Resolved: that cigarette smoking is hazardous to health" is a proposition of factual judgment; and "Resolved: that the best films being made today are French films" is a proposition of value judgment.

A **factual judgment** relates to reality and deals with either past, present, or future fact. If you were to argue that "Wage and price controls were a primary method used to control inflation during World War II," you would be arguing past fact. An example of present factual judgment is to argue that "Present inflation trends can be controlled without involving wage and price controls." A future factual argument might be: "By the year 2000 every American citizen will be insured for all medical costs." On the other hand, arguing that "Cigarette smoking is hazardous to health" is an example of a factual argument that might well be classified as belonging in all three categories—past, present, and future fact.

Value judgments are qualitative judgments, an assertion as to the worth of a concept, a person, or a thing. Unlike with a proposition of fact, you cannot evaluate a proposition as an objective statement uninfluenced by emotion, surmise, or personal prejudice. **Qualitative judgments** are by necessity abstract judgments. They do not deal with concrete existence but rather with concepts usually worded in abstruse terms—words such as "good," "bad," "wrong," "best," "beauty," "truth," "justice," and "moral"—and, thus, cannot be verified empirically.

The second type of proposition, the one most used in tournament debate, is the **policy** proposition. This type concerns future action and calls for a change from the way things are presently done. For example, topics such as, "Resolved: that the Federal government should establish minimum educational standards for elementary and secondary schools in the United States," or "Resolved: that the Federal government should significantly curtail the powers of labor unions in the United States," call for future action and are policy propositions. You can almost always recognize policy propositions by the inclusion of the term "should", which implies that a particular course of action ought to be pursued.

The first task you should do in **proposition analysis**, then, is to identify the proposition as to type: judgment (fact/value) or policy.

Interpreting the Proposition

Once the proposition is worded and classified, its crucial terms must be defined. The wording of an academic proposition is frequently broad because it concerns a topic of sufficient timeliness and depth to be debated nationally for an academic year. Consequently, by its very nature it lends itself to a variety of interpretations. However, broad or narrow, it is imperative, if there is to be a meaningful debate, that the affirmative and negative teams accept a reasonably similar definition of terms for the proposition. Your first impulse may be to reach for a dictionary and look up any words whose meanings are uncertain. While in some instances this would be a good basis on which to operate; in others it could result in a distorted interpretation of the resolution depending on which meaning you chose. For instance, the dictionary offers at least ten different meanings for that much used word LOVE— from (1) an intense affection for another person based on familial or personal ties to (10) a zero score in tennis.

Sometimes you must define not only individual words in the resolution, but the phrases in which they are used. If you carefully read and examine the topic, you should discover instances in which the meaning of a phrase goes beyond the meanings of its component words.

A good method of interpreting the resolution is to read what the experts in the field have to say. Eminent authorities will use synonyms for the terms of the proposition, discuss its history, make comparisons, and will often indicate what a term does not mean. By sticking with what the experts believe, debaters will not only be on surer ground in terms of definition but will be more solidly based when it comes time to do intensive research.

When the meaning of the topic is relatively clear, you should begin to explore the background of the question in order to determine where we are, how we got there, and why the question under consideration is crucial at this point in time. Most propositions chosen for academic debate have a long history, but usually are brought to the fore by a recent occurrence. To interpret the question properly, you should know both the origins of the controversy and the reasons for its current importance. Understanding why a problem has long existed without solution may give excellent clues to arguments which will become crucial during the season. So familiarize yourself with the history of this problem. How long has it been a problem area? What has happened to cause it to be the proposition for debate this year?

Controlling the Issues

With the proposition interpreted, the debater must discover the important issues which are contained in the proposition. You may define an issue as a crucial question, affirmed by the affirmative and denied by the negative, on whose acceptance depends the outcome of the debate. Those affirming the proposition have no choice but to prove each issue not admitted or waived by those opposing the proposition; the opponents need win but one issue to overcome the proposition. A simple way to illustrate the role of issues in a proposition is to turn to the common law definition of the crime of burglary. To be guilty of burglary a person must be guilty of five essential items: (1) breaking and (2) entering (3) a dwelling (4) at night (5) with felonious intent.[2] If the proposition were "Mr. X is guilty of burglary," the prosecution must prove all five items while the defense needs to disprove only one. If the prosecution loses one issue, it loses the case. Mr. X might then be guilty of something, but not burglary. Unfortunately, while the propositions you debate aren't usually as simple as the one in this example, nor are the issues as clearly prescribed, the principle is the same: The advocates must discover the inherent pivotal points in the proposition in order to build the strongest possible case.

Debaters should be aware of the various types of issues. Authorities usually classify issues as potential, admitted, actual, and stock. **Potential issues** are those inherent in the proposition. These potential issues are the same for any debater analyzing a particular proposition, as they exist independent of the whims of the advocate. They are not to be invented, but to be discovered. These are the issues every debater who desires to build the strongest possible case on the proposition must prepare to debate.

It is safe to say that in most debates you will not argue all the potential issues. For reasons of convenience or time those opposing the proposition may admit on waiver certain issues which will thus be dropped from the debate. For example, an insurance salesman may be attempting to sell a life insurance policy; the proposition would be "Ms. X admits she needs more coverage; the policy is obviously good; and she can afford it; but she concludes that she would rather spend her money in some other way." In this real life debate there are three **admitted issues** and one actual issue; the decision rests on the advantage of using the money in another way.

Actual issues, then, are those which remain in the debate after the admitted issues have been dropped from contention. You should understand that the proposition's opponents actually control the issues debated and that the advocates of the proposition have the burden of proving all issues not admitted or waived. It can be very embarrassing to an advocate who has not done a thorough analysis when the opposition introduces an issue on which that advocate is not prepared to debate. Analyzing the proposition for all potential issues and being well prepared to debate each of them is an obligation no debater can afford to shirk.

Finally, there are the **stock issues**. These can prove most helpful as a starting point in the analysis of propositions. The emphasis here must be on the phrase "starting point," for stock issues are not units of arguments, but are, rather, stages of analysis through which the advocate should go in developing the case. As an early step in the analysis, stock issues have been recognized and used by advocates since Hermogenes in the Second Century A.D. As an advocate, you should avoid substituting stock issues for the hard thinking and thorough analysis required for discovering all potential issues. Especially for the beginning debater, however, the stock issues can prove to be a helpful starting point in the analysis of the proposition.

The phrasing of the issues or their exact number for policy propositions may vary from author to author, but usually the modern list contains four:

1. Is there a problem which requires change? (Ill)
2. What is the cause of this problem? (Blame)
3. Is there a plan to solve the problem? (Cure)
4. Are there other disadvantages to this plan? (Cost)

The first stock issue raises questions concerning significant past, present, or future harms; do they exist and what is being done about them? In other words, is there significant harm present that calls for some type of action to be taken?

The second stock issue attempts to isolate the cause of the difficulty, since it is often impossible to solve a problem whose genesis is unknown. Here you are attempting to determine as exactly as possible who or what deserves the blame for this problem.

Thirdly, it must be discovered if there is a solution to the problem; it does little good to try to change if there is no effective means available to solve the problem. We have diagnosed the illness and its causes; now what is the prescribed cure?

Fourth, the ramifications of the change being proposed must be considered. Many plans sound good, and may actually solve the problem, but while doing so may create more difficulties than they eliminate. In other words, is this the best possible solution?

The stock issues for judgment propositions are two in number:

1. Does the proposition suggest specific criteria that can be used as questions to establish the truth or worth of the judgment?
2. Do the answers to these criteria questions establish the judgment as one to be accepted?

In the factual proposition, "Resolved: that cigarette smoking is hazardous to health," certain criteria questions become obvious: (1) Are there ingredients in cigarette smoke which are known to have harmful effects? (2) If so, which ones and to what extent? (3) Can smoking, *per se*, be isolated as a harmful effect?

The value proposition, "Resolved: that the best films being made today are French films," would suggest you start a search for criteria by which to measure the worth of the films being considered: (1) What components are essential to make a film one of superior quality? (2) Which of these components are stronger in French films than in other films? (3) Which of these components are stronger in non-French films? (4) Comparing strengths and weaknesses, are French films superior overall?

Again, stock issues are not the only way to discover all the issues in a given proposition. After all, no formal scheme of analysis can provide all the questions needed to be asked in search for issues, but they are an excellent place to start in your analysis of a proposition. They can usually save a good deal of time.

In any issues analysis, an additional area merits investigation—the **value assumptions** underlying the subject. **Values** are standards people set up to measure good or bad, right or wrong; and they frequently determine the way we think and talk about a subject. The debater should try to discover what values are at work in the pro and con arguments discovered in the analysis research. Consider such controversies as comprehensive medical care, child care, public housing, gun control, or abortion on demand, to name a few. If there is any doubt that value judgments are frequently intertwined with policy judgments, a listing of the issues on any of the topics mentioned should quickly put that doubt to rest.

For example, one of the most controversial problems being argued in this country is "abortion on demand," brought to the forefront by the United States Supreme Court declaring it a constitutional right for a woman to choose to have an abortion. The overall proposition being debated is a proposition of policy: "Resolved: that abortion should be made an illegal act." However, the issues come down to two value arguments: (1) the right of a woman to control whether she may end a pregnancy versus (2) the rights of an unborn child. No matter how the original proposition of policy is worded, pro-choice and pro-life groups are debating a proposition of value, "Abortion is bad."

However, a complete analysis does not end here. All value judgments actually assume the existence of certain facts. So having discovered the value induced issues, you then will want to discover the underlying **factual assumptions**. In the abortion argument, it appears that the basis for the anti-abortion value issue, that abortion is wrong, is based on the factual assumption that life begins at the moment of conception; therefore abortion is ending the life of a child. The pro-abortion stand seems to be based on the factual assumption that women have a right to the control over their bodies based on long accepted American values which are constitutionally protected.[3]

While all policy propositions may not be as emotionally entrapped in value judgments as is the one concerning abortion, it is difficult to find a policy proposition not involving value judgments. The debater who understands the values underlying policy questions has stolen a march on the opposition and is in a much better position to debate the proposition.

New Approaches to
Interpreting the Proposition

In the early 1970's some debate theorists introduced a type of investigation called "systems analysis." **Systems analysis** is based on the theory that any system is an assembly of parts that by interaction or interdependence function as a whole. It attempts to study the interacting parts as a complete entity, but recognizes that all systems are in a constant process of change— they cannot be given static boundaries or limits— and are, by their very nature, highly dependent on human judgment. Therefore, these debate theorists argue that propositions are not subject to regular cause-effect relations or to analysis as though static in nature, but require an approach such as systems analysis.

Brock and others maintain that, "With the stock issue approach to analysis the central issues are the present conditions and the causes of those conditions. Thus, the affirmative's responsibility to establish the probability of specific future conditions is minimal. However, with systems analysis the central issues are the action and the effects of the action, so the affirmative must establish probability of the future effects of the proposed system."[4] They suggest that a structural analysis of an open system can be provided by examining four concepts: components, relationships, effects, and goals.[5]

Ziegelmueller and Dause summarize well the role of systems analysis as originally conceived:

> In sum, the systems approach provides an inductive model which is optimally useful for analysis of controversies which have not yet been focused on a specific course of action. As a tool for the analysis of policy controversies it should be thought of as complementing the stock issues formula rather than as an alternative to stock issues. It is possible, and frequently desirable, to use the two formulas together.
>
> . . . . Systems analysis, with its focus on the relationships of interdependent components within a system can provide useful insight into the nature of an existing system even within the framework of stock issue analysis.[6]

While systems analysis and stock issues analysis are similar in that both are useful means of deciding on a specific policy and can be used together, theorists soon widened the distinctions between the two methods, creating a growing difference of opinion on how a proposition should be analyzed, debated, and judged. Several differing theories emerged from the systems analysis concept. The two most frequently being debated in the forensics literature and actual debates are policy systems analysis and hypothesis testing. Both are theoretical concepts with the stated aim of giving debate participants a more real life problem-solving activity than can be claimed for the traditional stock issues approach.

The basic differences between the stock issues approach and that of policy systems analysis and hypothesis testing can be summed up as follows:

Stock Issues Analysis prescribes a set of rules (stock issues) as the starting basis for determining whether or not a policy resolution should be accepted. Advocates are arguing whether or not the particular problem-solution approach being offered by the affirmative should be accepted as the reason for change and, thus, acceptance of the stated proposition. The presumption lies with the negative; the burden of proof is on the affirmative.

Policy Systems Analysis does not limit the debate to one particular problem-solution for adoption of the proposition. The premise upon which this analysis system is built is that any policy adopted should be tested against an alternative policy. As applied to scholastic debate, policy systems analysis has resulted in the affirmative arguing for the adoption of a specific course of action (policy) as identified by the affirmative plan, with the negative introducing a counterplan advocating another specific course of action (policy) differing from that of the affirmative. This results in the negative arguing that the affirmative policy should be rejected in favor of the negative policy, with the judge making a comparison between the two policies and deciding which should be selected. The policy systems analysis model eliminates the traditional concept of the burden of proof being with the affirmative and presumption with the negative. Based on the theory that change is an ongoing process, the presumption is that change is inevitable and not debatable; consequently, both teams have an equal burden of proof.

For example, say the proposition for debate is: "Resolved: that abortion should be made an illegal act in the United States." The affirmative builds its case on the factual assumption that life begins at the moment of conception, therefore abortion is ending the life of a child. In an attempt to limit the options of the negative, the main thrust of the affirmative plan is the saving of a million innocent lives each year. The negative does not challenge the factual assumption of the affirmative, nor does it challenge the affirmative figures, but counterplans with an international program to end famine in the world thus saving the lives of several million children. The negative proposal is based on four arguments: (1) Millions more children are dying from famine than from U.S. abortions; (2) For famine to be controlled and these lives saved the U.S. has to be the major provider; (3) If the U.S. population is allowed to increase a million or more a year by outlawing abortion, the U.S. would be unable to contribute sufficiently to end world famine; and (4) More lives would be saved by adopting the negative proposal.

The policy systems analysis concept has enjoyed wide acceptance, particularly on the college level. Others have strongly condemned it for leading to a proliferation of narrow affirmative interpretations of the proposition, an automatic-weapons-fire rate of delivery and spewing of arguments— all sins attributable to crowding an unsuitable system into traditional debate time limits. But whatever its strengths or weaknesses, policy systems analysis is a fact of debate life and must be considered when analyzing a policy proposition.

Hypothesis Testing as a debate model was introduced as a means of using argumentation to test the truth of a proposition. Modeled after the scientific method of hypothesis testing, it construes presumption as "not in favor of maintaining the present system, but against the specific resolution being argued."[7] It must be kept in mind that the audience (judge) is being asked to accept the probable truth or value of the proposition, not to adopt it. Where the policy systems analysis requires the acceptance of one policy over another, hypothesis testing requires only accepting or rejecting the probable truth of the affirmative hypothesis.

Unlike policy systems analysis where the affirmative offers one policy plan and the negative counters with another, hypothesis testing places no limits on the number of positions a negative may offer. Thus, a negative may offer several, even hypothetical and inconsistent counterplan positions, since the best way to test a hypothesis is to compare it with as many alternative hypotheses as possible.

Let us say the proposition for debate is: "Resolved: that Congress should make abortion an illegal act in the United States." Under the hypothesis testing concept the negative might respond to the affirmative by presenting two plans: (1) Appeal to the United States

Supreme Court to overturn *Roe v. Wade*; and (2) A Constitutional amendment making abortion illegal. They also argue a disadvantage consequence to the affirmative plan that contradicts the two negative plans, "Illegal abortions will offer serious consequences: (1) Many more women will die from illegal abortions than do under the safe conditions presently available; and (2) Hospital and medical costs resulting from women having had illegal abortions will soar." These approaches are acceptable to a hypothesis judge due to the concept that "the best way to test a hypothesis is to compare it with as many alternative hypotheses as possible."

Hypothesis testing has its adherents, but more critics. It has not gained the level of acceptance of stock issues or policy systems analysis. The system is less frequently used, and, when used, is frequently misconstrued by debaters and judges as a form of policy system analysis.[8]

Whatever mode of analysis is used, or whether a combination of types is employed, analysis is truly the bedrock upon which cases are built. Only by thorough analysis of the proposition can advocates hope to discover those pivotal points— the issues— which are so essential to the eventual success of their efforts. However, we do suggest that no matter which system is finally used to build the case, the initial starting point should be with stock issues.

The editor of the script of a championship round of the National Debate Tournament once asked the question, "Could it be that our propositions are too broad or our interpretations too narrow?" No matter how this question is answered, debaters should opt for what they believe to be the most reasonable interpretation of the proposition—reasonable being defined as an interpretation likely to be accepted if they were to debate the proposition before an audience of non-experts on debate. To do so seems more likely to produce a debate whose outcome will be determined by issues inherent in the proposition than by strategic forensic techniques.

NOTES

1. Walter F. Terris, "The Classification of the Argumentative Proposition: *The Quarterly Journal of Speech,* XLIX (October, 1963), pp. 266-273.
2. McBurney, O'Neill, Mills, *Argumentation and Debate:Techniques of a Free Society* (New York: The MacMillan Company, 1951), p. 31.
3. A good discussion of the analysis of propositions of value judgment may be found in Ronald J. Matlon, "Debating Propositions of Value," *Journal of the American Forensic Association,* XIV, 4 (Spring, 1978), pp. 194-204.
4. Brock, Chesebro, Cragan, Klumpp, *Public Policy Decision Making: Systems Analysis and Comparative Advantage Debate* (New York: Harper and Row, 1973), p. 162.
5. ibid., p. 38.
6. George Ziegelmueller and Charles Dause, *Argumentation, Inquiry and Advocacy* (Englewood Cliffs, New Jersey: Prentice Hall, 1975), p. 42.
7. Jerome R. Corsi, "Zarefsky's Theory of Debate as Hypothesis Testing: A Critical Re-examination: *Journal of the American Forensic Association,* XIX (Winter, 1983), p. 158.
8. Enlightening discussions of the pros and cons of the policy systems analysis and hypothesis testing concepts can be found in: "Special Forum: *The Hypothesis Testing Program,*" *Journal of the American Forensic Association,* XIX, 3 (Winter, 1983), pp. 158-190. "A Forum on Policy Systems Analysis," *Journal of the American Forensic Association,* XXII, 3 (Winter, 1986), pp. 125-175.

4
CHAPTER

Research

In many ways this is the most important chapter of this book. While many of the skills you learn in debate—organization, analysis, communication—will stand you in good stead throughout your academic career and beyond, the ability to research well has more general application than any other. This is especially true since a large proportion of those who debate seriously go on into the law or academia—two fields where research is paramount.

The Process of Research

After analyzing the proposition and discerning its component issues, you should determine exactly what resources are avail able. The best way to accomplish this is to prepare a comprehensive **bibliography**. Taking the list of issues or areas which the proposition covers, you should proceed to the library and use the various bibliographic aids (discussed in this chapter) to make a list of every source available on the resolution. While this may appear to be a tremendous task and is rarely achieved by any debate squad on any topic, it should nonetheless be held up as the ideal for which to strive. How else will you know what is available? If you do not compose a complete list of the potential resources, then you may miss many valuable items. Therefore, initial comprehensiveness is essential.

Secondly, you should categorize the materials according to their estimated value. Some items will, from their author or title, spring out from the prepared list; their value will be immediately obvious. Others will seem less worthwhile; some will seem of little importance. By beginning with the most valuable works, you will absorb the most crucial material while you are still "fresh" on the topic and have the most time to spend. While you may miss a few good items, a careful analysis of the bibliography should uncover a majority of the most important works.

Next, the materials to be copied should be read and marked. It is difficult initially to know what will be of great value and what will not; for this reason you should mark a large number of items before actually sitting down to type your cards. In this way you will become more familiar with what is available and may discover that some of the earliest material was apparently worthless or redundant and need not be "carded."

Debaters should not be concerned at the start about what type of affirmative case will be employed or how each card will be used on the negative; to do so will merely waste time and perhaps cause you to miss something of great value simply because its use cannot be anticipated. Simply accumulate! It is undoubtedly true that some material will later be found to be worthless, but it is far better to have taken one hundred cards and never use them than to have missed five cards that will be needed desperately the next February. Only after the initial flurry of gathering is done and you know where the topic is tending, should you start to consider the use of each item. Experienced debaters who use the time before school starts in the fall to the best advantage will reap great dividends later in the year. If you cover all the basics—and with luck even a bit more—by September 1, you can use the time during the year to keep up with current material and research those inevitable "**squirrels**" (unorthodox cases). If there is still a lot of elementary research to be done when classes begin, realistic hopes for a successful year are practically non-existent. It is no exaggeration to say that championships are won, or lost, during the summer of the preceding year.

Finally, a word should be said about the basis of affirmative cases. Many debaters, from the beginner to the advanced performer, hear the topic, do a bit of reading, and come up with the "unbeatable" affirmative case. This, of course, is doing the job backwards. Like a competent scientist in the laboratory or, more exactly, like a social scientist conducting a poll, the debater should not base research on ideas, but should make sure to base ideas on research. After discovering what the topic means, what the experts have said, and what the evidence most strongly proves, you are ready to establish the most powerful arguments for the adoption of the proposition. You are not ready before such an examination.

Sources of Material

There are numerous **sources** of debate material, but let us concentrate on the six most productive: books, periodicals, newspapers, pamphlets, government documents, and online resources.

• Books

Books are often the first source to which the debater turns for an overall understanding of the topic. They are especially good for background material and in-depth studies of some aspect of the subject. Many debaters begin by going immediately to the card catalogue of the library and exploring the list of books it contains. This, however, is in conflict with the "comprehensive" philosophy discussed above, for no library contains all the books on a particular topic. Rather, you should start with a bibliographic work which includes a vast number of the books available, such as *Books in Print*. Tᵢhis item, as its name implies, is a listing of all the books currently in print in the United States. From this work the book section of the bibliography may be constructed, and you can consult the catalogue of the local library to see which volumes that institution holds and which will need to be acquired from some other source.

In using books you must take great care to ensure that this one type of material does not consume all the research time available. Books are often several hundred pages long; there may be scores of them on a topic; and unless you are an exceptional speed reader, the chance of getting through them and having time left for anything else is very remote. Still, there are ways to use books without reading every word they contain. First, employ the table of contents to see if some of the chapters are irrelevant to the subject at hand. Next, check the index for key words and phrases; this will indicate sections of the book which contain the most helpful material. Finally, do not try to devour the work as carefully as a textbook; instead skim, again looking for key words and phrases. Rather than reading entire paragraphs employ their topic sentences as aids. Although important material may occasionally be missed, it is likely that you will find most of the good evidence, and save vital time.

As with any research material, books have strengths and weaknesses; the greatest strength is depth.   With the length of the average book, a writer may go into great detail, produce considerable evidence to support a point, and explain the reasoning fully. In no other type of material will you find such depth of coverage. On the other side of the coin, you must be aware of both amount and recency. The very extensiveness of a book may entrap you into over-using one source. So much good material may seem to exist in a book that you may take hundreds of cards on the one narrow aspect of the topic which the book covers; resist this temptation to go overboard. In addition, books may contain outdated material, much of it older than the copyright date on the work. A book published in 1989, for example, might well contain data collected as far back as 1985; the recency of material from older books should be checked.

• Periodicals

A second valuable source of material is periodicals. These exist in numerous types, ranging from the popular mass circulation journals— *Newsweek, Time, U. S. News*— to the highly technical and specialized journals of specific academic or professional fields. There are numerous bibliographic aids to help the re-searcher; the most common, and probably the first source which most beginning debaters learn, is the *Reader's Guide to Periodical Literature.* This index lists by subject, author, and title articles in just about all the popular journals plus a few of the more technical ones, such as *Science.* It is a very helpful source for general reading, but as soon as the material waxes technical, *Reader's Guide*'s usefulness drops off considerably. Then you need to turn to more comprehensive or more specific bibliographies. One of considerable usefulness is the *Bulletin of the Public Affairs Information Service,* or *PAIS* for short. This is much like the *Reader's Guide,* but it is much more extensive, covering not only vast numbers of periodicals but also some books and government documents as well. Finally, there are the technical aids in specific fields, such as the abstracts to publications in education or psychology, or the *Index to Legal Periodicals,* an item of great use to debaters.

When reading periodicals, you should spend as much time as possible with the advanced or technical journals. Mass circulation magazines are good for general background or for gaining an understanding of the current state of the subject, but they are too oriented to the public at large to be of great value to the debater. Journals also have several advantages, the most important of which is timeliness. A journal may impart knowledge only a week old; thus the debater may keep up with current developments in the field. In addition, it is in magazines that many important discoveries first make their public appearance. In the scientific fields such as medicine or technology, the reports of experimental results may be of vital importance in debate. Journals have disadvantages, however. The first of these is lack of depth. Even in some of the technical magazines, and certainly in the popular ones, lack of space precludes an extensive discussion of the reasons behind the conclusions reached. Thus, you may find a conclusion but no real evidence to support it save the credentials, if any, of the author. Another difficulty in periodicals is **bias**. Many journals have editorial policies which they push mercilessly. Take, for example, a story reported in both the *New Republic* and the *National Review*; one often would be hard pressed to recognize it as the same item. Nevertheless, with some care in choice and use, journals may prove a most valuable source of debate evidence.

• Newspapers

The third area of importance is newspapers. These extend all the way from the rural county weekly to the huge international which produces several issues daily. Finding items in newspapers is easier than might at first be thought, since two of the major American papers, the *New York Times* and the *Wall Street Journal*, publish their own indices. Organized much like the *Reader's Guide*, these direct the reader to the correct section, page, and column for the article sought. These are also valuable guides to other papers as well, since an important story would likely be in other papers on the same day it appeared in the *New York Times*.

Newspapers are like periodicals, except more so; they offer the same advantages and disadvantages except they are more extreme in the offering. They are the most timely source of material; if it happened yesterday, it can be found in the paper today. The wise debate squad subscribes to a national paper such as the *New York Times* in order to keep up with the progress of the topic. Yet at the same time the difficulty of brevity is exacerbated. Newspapers, even more than journals, are bound by the difficulty of too little space and have the additional problem of needing to meet time deadlines. Thus, in-depth coverage of a subject is rare. Papers harbor biases as well, some of which are extreme. Most major papers have lost the flagrant partisanship which existed in the last century, but many continue to editorialize on the front page and insert their own views into the reporting of stories. Be aware of the political and economic biases of the local paper; it may save embarrassing moments in a debate round.

• Pamphlets

A fourth and less well known source of material is pamphlets. These little booklets are generally published by organizations which have particular axes to grind and wish to draw the public to their side of a question. More than with any other source, you should use pamphlets with extreme care, since many of them are nothing more than outrageous **propaganda**. Nevertheless, they may well contain valuable policy statements or statistics virtually unobtainable elsewhere. On the consumer product safety topic once debated in college, for example, the automobile air bag case was very common; some of the best evidence on that case came from pamphlets prepared by various companies supporting air bag implementation. Obtain pamphlets, therefore, if only to refute the evidence others may have.

The two best sources of pamphlets are the library's vertical file and the publishers of the material themselves. The vertical file is a series of manila folders in which librarians place newspaper clippings, pamphlets, etc. on topics of current interest. This provides a good starting place in the hunt for booklets. If they are not obtainable there, you should write directly to the interested parties. Such organizations as the National Association of Manufacturers on one side of most questions and the AFL – CIO on the other are usually more than happy to supply their propaganda. If pamphlets are used carefully, one may occasionally find nuggets of gold among the mounds of mud.

• Government Documents

The most difficult, yet, many believe, the most valuable sources of information are U. S. Government publications. The federal government may well be the world's largest publishing house, turning out vast amounts of reading material. Finding exactly what you are looking for may be a task, but you can enlist the aid of two major bibliographic sources in your quest. The first is the *Monthly Catalogue of U. S. Government Publications*, a subject, author, and title index to the vast majority of the publications issued by Washington. The second is the index and abstract of the Congressional Information Service which, as the name suggests, lists Congressional material only. Nevertheless, it is of great help since Congress provides the majority of debate oriented material and because the abstract allows a foreknowledge of what the document contains.

Obtaining a desired document may prove a considerable task; however, there are several ways to proceed. A large number of publications are placed in depositories. Large libraries throughout the country, such as state libraries, those at major universities and in major cities, are designated government depositories. Each of these receives at least one copy of each deposited document. The debater should identify the depository in his area. If the needed document is not deposited, you may often obtain it from your Representative or Senator; especially in election years such individuals are eager to be of assistance. A few works are not free but must instead be purchased from the Superintendent of Documents in Washington. If such is the case, that information, plus the purchase price, will be noted in the *Monthly Catalogue*.

While the government issues vast amounts of material, such as reports of commissions, annual reports of agencies, etc., the most valuable items for debaters come from

Congress; and the most valuable Congressional documents are the *Congressional Record* (the verbatim report of the day-to-day debates and actions on the floor of both houses) and the records of Congressional hearings. Unless the squad contains someone who is an absolute glutton for research, an attempt to keep up each day with the *Congressional Record* is more trouble than it is worth. While you can undoubtedly find items of value in this journal, it also contains vast amounts of trash. The best way to utilize this source is to search for specific material using the index to the *Record*.

In all likelihood, the most valuable single source available to debaters is the record of Congressional hearings. Whenever Congress undertakes to pass important legislation, hearings are held, witnesses called, and a thorough examination of the proposal is made. In using such hearings considerable caution must be exercised. First, as with a book, it is probably counterproductive to read all the way through a hearing; there is too much of little use located among the valuable materials. Rather, use the table of contents and examine the **credentials** of witnesses. In almost all hearings, many witnesses are called who have little or no expertise on the subject; they are called, individually or as representatives of influential groups, simply as a matter of courtesy. It may be very diplomatic of Congress to request the opinion of management, labor, church groups, and the League of Women Voters; however, in many instances what these people have to say is virtually worthless for debate purposes. Concentrate instead on the professionals, the academicians, and those who have spent their lives working with or studying the problem at hand; these are the people who will say what is worthwhile.

There is also duplication in hearings. Many individuals bring written statements which are simply inserted in the record; they then are asked to make an oral statement, which is often merely an abridgment of the written document; and then they are questioned about what they have said. One should not make the mistake of reading the same material over and over again. In addition, the same individuals often testify before both Senate and House committees on the same bill and will almost certainly say about the same thing before each. One reading is enough. Do not, however, make the error of skipping over the questioning; like cross-examination in a debate, it can often make clear the obfuscated and expose embarrassing inconsistencies in the witness' prepared statements. A little reading in the questioning may prove worth its weight in gold if you can later discredit a source used by an opposition speaker who has done a less thorough job of research.

Finally, the federal is only one of the levels of government. Both the states and international agencies, such as the United Nations, also produce large numbers of documents. These may be of great value if the topic addresses a specific concern of such an agency.

• On-Line Resources

As technology leaps forward, more and more researchers are coming to rely on computerized approaches to discovering and developing their material. Such resources, usually referred to as "on-line" sources, can help you develop your bibliography and evidence files.

In some libraries the assistance of a librarian may be required when you use the computer facilities. In other institutions you may be free to utilize the on-line resources individually. Among the sources which a debater may wish to check are the following:

• *ASI (American Statistics Index)*. This provides governmental statistical information.
• CIS. A computerized version of the Congressional Information Service referred to above.
• *Magazine Index*. A computerized version of the *Reader's Guide*.
• *National Newspaper Index*. A guide to articles in the major national newspapers.
• VU/TEXT. This provides actual texts of various newspapers, encyclopedias, etc.

As this research area develops and expands, it will offer more extensive facilities to debaters. Computerized data bases are constantly growing and changing. It is a good idea to consult the staff at the libraries you use most frequently to see what resources are available to you.

Note Taking

Several comments should be made on the taking of evidence from all the above sources. The desired quotation should be recorded on an index card; the exact size of the card is pretty much a matter of personal preference, although most high school and college debaters now use 4 x 6 inches.

The evidence card consists of two major parts: the bibliographic data and the body of the evidence itself. The bibliographic material must be sufficient to allow you to easily rediscover the original citation. It should include the name of the *author* (if there is one as with a book) or the person speaking (as in a Congressional hearing); his *credentials*; the *title* of the work (or the name of the magazine); the *date* of the statement (or publication date of the book or magazine); and the *page* (with newspapers the section and column numbers). You need not, of course, read all of this when presenting the evidence in a debate, but all of it should be on the card for verification of the source if such is demanded.

The evidence itself should be taken precisely as it appeared in the original, even to lack of correct grammar, punctuation, or spelling, if such occurred. The proper way to indicate such error in the original is to place the word **[sic]** (Latin for "thus") in brackets— not parentheses— after the error; this tells a reader that the mistake was in the original. When the exact context of the material is not clear form the quotation, insert a word, such as a noun, to make clear the referent of a pronoun. How many of us have heard an "it" in a statement without having the foggiest notion of what "it" was? In this case also enclose the interpolation in brackets to indicate that it is an addition.

Sometimes two parts of what you wish to quote are separated by material which is unnecessary for debate purposes. It is perfectly permissible to omit such material, *provided it does not change the meaning of the quotation.* The proper way to indicate omissions in a quotation is through the use of elipses— three spaced dots if less than a sentence is omitted, or four dots, the first following the word and the other three spaced, if more than a sentence is omitted. Be careful not to copy lengthy quotations. Not only is some of the material probably unnecessary, but trying to read a long quotation at spread speed is often the most counterproductive of debate actions.

Some debaters believe that it is permissible to **paraphrase** a quotation as long as the original intent of the author is maintained. While this is probably academically defensible, a number of judges frown on the practice; so be aware that you paraphrase at your own risk. If the paraphrase is used, indicate so on the card and take extra care not to do violence to the original intent of the author.

Organizing the Filebox

After the material has been researched and recorded on cards, you face one of the most onerous tasks in the preparation process— organizing your file box. If you have researched thoroughly, you will have accumulated thousands of pieces of evidence which to be usable must be filed in a logical manner so that you may identify and retrieve them at a moment's notice during the heat of a debate round.

The organizing process is best done by teams, with both members taking part. Debaters should set aside a considerable block of time—an evening, for example. They should begin by going through their accumulated material card by card, looking at each one and then placing it in one of a dozen or so piles according to the major issue or area of the topic to which it relates. Some debaters tend to organize first into affirmative and negative; while this may be a reasonable approach, it ignores the distinct possibility that some cards may relate to both sides of the topic. Once you have separated the cards, subdivide each large pile, using the same process. Depending on the amount of evidence, even a third reading and division may be necessary. When all this has been accomplished, the debaters should be faced with a large number of small piles, each containing at most ten to fifteen pieces of evidence.

Each card must now be numbered.

Many debaters use a letter-number-letter system (such as A–12–f), where the initial letter stands for the original large pile (representing a major area of the proposition), the number for the smaller division of that issue, and the final letter for the specific card. This system not only facilitates finding the material during the round, but it also greatly aids refiling after the debate is over. As a final step, make an index indicating how the file box is organized. Use dividers to separate the various groups of cards within the box.

A subsidiary benefit from this process is that having read over each card as many as three times you will have gained a relatively clear idea of what evidence you possess; this will be most valuable when deciding on the proper affirmative case to espouse and when wondering during a debate whether a certain argument can be supported with evidence. Thus, although the organizing process can be a major task, it will produce benefits to the student who undertakes it conscientiously.

As we mentioned at the start of this chapter, skill in research may be the most important skill debate can teach. Certainly we have not herein explored all of the sources and techniques open to the researcher; but if you master these basics, you will have a thorough foundation for success, not only in this activity but in many others as well.

5

CHAPTER

Evidence

Bernard Baruch once said, "Every man has a right to his own opinion, but no man has a right to be wrong in his facts." This statement should be a commandment to those who participate in debate. Whether or not the evidence introduced to support an argument says what the advocate claims it does is a matter of personal integrity; the ethical debater makes every effort to be certain the supporting material used is precisely what it is implied to be.

Evidence as used in academic debate traditionally consists of facts, opinions, and material objects used to support contentions. Evidence differs from reasoning, the other component of proof, in that evidence is separate from the advocate— something that must be found outside oneself. Reasoning, on the other hand, is a part of the advocate— an invention of the mind. Evidence is the starting point of argument— the material from which we reason. The quantity and quality of the evidence available to build the case is solely dependent on the completeness of the research done on the proposition.

In the chapter, let us first discuss the types of evidence available to the advocate and then consider the tests of evidence.

The Types of Evidence

As noted, evidence is said to consist of facts, opinions, and material things. **Factual evidence** consists of presumably verifiable statements that are not subject to opinion judgments. Factual evidence concerns some event, circumstance, or phenomenon that has happened or is happening, the occurrence of which can be proven. It is introduced into the debate in the form of statistical data, historical happenings, or specific examples. What makes it a distinct form of evidence is that it is free of interpretation or judgment. When a television meteorologist predicts rain for the weekend, even though that individual is an expert and every other expert using the same data would predict the same results, the prediction is not a fact. It is only an expert opinion that there is a high degree of probability that it will rain during the weekend. It is a fact that rain has been predicted; it is a fact that the predictor has a high statistical record of being correct; but until the rain falls, precipitation is not a fact.

Opinion evidence is derived from the testimony of witnesses who are classified as either *expert* or *ordinary* witnesses. The expert witness is one who by special training or experience is qualified not only to present factual material but also to interpret it. The expert witness is one who testifies from particular personal knowledge that it is the opinion of the witness that the material in question is true. An ordinary witness is one who can testify that something is true because the witness observed it to be so. The trained weather meteorologist is an expert witness whose opinion that it will rain on the planned picnic day is based on specialized training and experience in interpreting certain specific data. Uncle George, who may disagree with the expert witness because "his corn isn't throbbing and it always throbs when it is going to rain," is an ordinary witness. Which opinion an audience will accept will depend upon which source has the higher degree of credibility with the listeners.

Material objects are known in the law as real evidence—evidence that consists of tangible objects. In educational debate, material objects consist of items ranging from the actual primary evidence source to visual aids. Debaters will often read from the book or journal in which an appropriate quotation appears, or debaters may introduce the book or article from which an opponent has claimed to quote and demand verification of the quotation. Likewise, visual aids can clarify a point. A few years ago, a college affirmative team advocating the addition of a particular safety device to all firearms used a mock-up of a revolver to demonstrate the feasibility of the device. The use of material things as evidence can add authenticity and clarity to the supporting material and thus aid in gaining the desired belief.

Evidence consists of facts, opinions, and material things. It is the starting point of argument— the material from which we reason.

The Tests of Evidence

There are two major tests that you should apply to any piece of evidence: the test of **quantity** and the test of **quality**. The purpose of the quantity test is to make certain that a sufficient amount of support has been offered to verify the contention. Here should be asked such questions as:

1. Have several authorities been cited?
2. Have the citations been derived from more than one source?
3. Have one, a few, or several examples been offered in support of the contention?

In other words, has enough evidence been offered to support the contentions so that reasonable people would accept them as true?

In testing the quality of the evidence, one should examine source, recency, and relevancy to determine the reliability of the evidence being used. Testing the **source** is the first and most important test to make of any piece of evidence. If it is factual evidence, is the source noted for *expertise, accuracy,* and *thoroughness*? If it is a purported factual study: (1) Who financed the study? (2) Why was it done? (3) How was it conducted? (4) Is there other evidence to corroborate each fact? (5) Is the information first hand? In other words, the first and basic test for any piece of evidence— fact, opinion, material object— is to determine who is responsible for the existence of the evidence and how do they know? Perhaps because this test is not always an easy one to apply, it is too frequently skipped.

Having verified the source, you then test the evidence for **recency**. In this day of constant research and ever expanding knowledge, the *date* of the evidence can be very important. Government policies change; new laws are passed; old laws are repealed; court cases are decided; and new discoveries are made— what may have been an excellent piece of evidence quickly can become obsolete. A favorite technique of many debaters is counteracting an opponent's quotation with a later dated source. The debater should be aware, however, that the new quotation may not be more recent evidence. A publication date is not always a reliable indication of recency. You should check the source of the statement, the date the study was made, and any other relevant material that will date the citation. It may turn out not to be as recent as implied. Good debaters keep their evidence up to date, both to advance their own arguments and retard those raised against them. Keep in mind that recency in itself does not necessarily make the evidence usable. Did it also pass the source test?

Relevancy is the third important test to establish the quality of the evidence. How relevant to the argument is the evidence? Does the evidence actually say what the advocate says it does? Is, perhaps, the best argument against it, "So what?"

Statistics

Somebody once said, "Figures don't lie, but liars figure." Keep this little saying in mind when dealing with statistics. **Statistics** are a distinct form of factual evidence that deserve special attention because they can be most helpful in developing arguments. Statistics can be excellent evidence. They are, by their very nature, multiple examples from which to generalize a statement; they can be effective means for comparison and contrast; and they are readily available. Whatever the position being argued, the odds are good there are statistics available to support the contention or to oppose it.

Statistics also deserve special attention because, intentionally or otherwise, they can manipulate and mislead the listener. As an advocate, you should be aware that because you read the statistics in a reputable source or heard them given by a respected national figure, this does not mean you do not need to check them for source, accuracy, and relevancy. Unfortunately, certain errors are all too common, and though the resultant statistics sound convincing, they actually are irrelevant to the argument. For instance, for years taxpayers and parents never doubted when a state's Department of Education reported that the students in that state had scored above the national average on the standardized tests for reading, writing, and arithmetic. Then somebody noticed that *all* the states were reporting that their students were testing above average. Since everybody cannot be above average, something had to be wrong with the figures. Something was wrong. The national testing service supplying the tests had determined the "average" by testing a sample group that included students with learning disabilities. Also, when this sample group had been tested to determine the average score, the students should have had to take all the tests that would be available to the school districts. However, when school districts administered the test, they could pick and choose those tests which best matched their curriculum. The consequent figures reported were valid figures for the test given, but the report was not relevant as to what "average" actually was.

There are several tests to apply to statistics to be certain they are relevant. First, statistics should be from a sample of adequate size and scope. When college teams were debating National Health Insurance, negative teams did well with a study claiming that about ninety-seven percent of retired people over sixty-five years of age could provide for their own medical expenses. This study did well, that is, until affirmative teams discovered that the survey covered only wealthy retired people in what appeared to be carefully selected retirement centers.

Another cause of irrelevant statistics is invalid comparative use of differing units of measurement. For instance, juvenile crime statistics are often misleading because states differ in crime definitions and age of juveniles. Some states classify running away from home as a juvenile crime; others do not classify a runaway as a juvenile criminal. Some states define juveniles as anyone under twenty-one years of age; other states use a variety of lower ages. A specific example of frequently quoted statistical studies that are not relevant comparisons are Standardized Aptitude Test (SAT) scores used to rank the states. The various states use differing units of measurement. For instance, the 1988 national average was reported to be a score of 904 on the possible 1600 on the combined verbal and math tests. As usual, Iowa was tops reporting a score of 1090. Indiana was well down the list with a score of 870. However, in Iowa only five percent of college bound students take the test, but in Indiana fifty-five percent of its college bound students take the test, and in Illinois ten percent of the students planning to apply for admission are tested. Add the fact that in some states there may be a greater percentage of various ethnic groups from a greater variety of social backgrounds, and another variable has been added to affect the relevancy of the statistics. So remember, be certain the statistical units you use or that are used against your case are clearly defined and comparable.

The careful debater always ascertains that the statistics used measure the item at issue. For instance, does the number of tax dollars spent per student measure the quality of education given? Does the percentage drop in employment in October indicate a forthcoming recession or is it merely a seasonal drop that may or may not signify an overall drop in employment? Are the statistics showing a higher average family income indicative of a stronger economy or more two income families? There is a common tendency to make a few simple statistics serve as the indicator of an entire complex economic situation or involved social problem. Make certain the statistics used are an index of what is being claimed.

Again, statistics can be excellent evidence. They are multiple examples from which to generalize a statement; they can be an effective means for comparison and contrast; but you should always check them for source, recency, and relevancy.

Summary

Evidence should be important to the audience debater; it is crucial to the competitive debater. As experienced debaters know well, debate decisions are so often won or lost by the presence or lack of that all-important piece of evidence. So, a speaker must have the needed evidence and be certain it will pass with honors the following test questions:

Does the evidence meet the test of quantity?
1. Is there more than one piece of evidence to support the contention? A sufficient number? Is the sample of adequate size and scope?
2. Is there more than one source of the evidence? Is there a diversity of sources?
3. Is this an isolated example or a typical example?

Does the evidence pass the test of quality?
1. Is the source susceptible to hard attack?
   a. Is the source trained in research?
   b. Has the source made a study?
   c. Is the source prejudiced?
   d. Is the source speaking against his/her own interests or beliefs?
   e. Is the source noted for reliability?
   f. Is the source consistent with previous statements or findings?
   g. Is the source in agreement with other reputable authorities in the field?

   h. Are there negative instances?
2. Is the evidence capable of passing the recency test?
   a. Is the material cited of recent date? The most recent date?
   b. Is the publication date a true indication of the recency of the material cited?
3. Is the evidence presented relevant to the item being supported?
   a. Does the evidence presented really prove the conclusion drawn from it?
   b. Is it an example of a few, some, many, all?
   c. If it is opinion evidence, does it present a reasonable interpretation of the evidence?
   d. If it is a quotation, has it been altered to make it more relevant?
   e. Are the statistics quoted relevant to the argument?
      (1) Is the sample of adequate size and scope?
      (2) Do the compared units of measurement differ?
      (3) Do the statistics measure the particular item at issue?

   To paraphrase Baruch, all debaters have a right to use any evidence they choose, but no debater has a right to misuse evidence to distort, deceive, or deliberately misrepresent.

6

CHAPTER

Reasoning

Cardinal Newman defined reasoning as any process by which the mind advances from knowing one thing to knowing another. Reasoning, then, is the process of drawing inferences from the available evidence (facts, opinions, and material objects). Evidence and reasoning combine to establish proof— proof being defined as that which serves to convince the mind that a fact or proposition is true. Reasoning is presented in a debate in units of proof called arguments. An argument must consist of a conclusion and at least one reason for accepting that conclusion. If you say to a friend, "The student body at Old Siwash is getting smarter— average scores on entrance exams are going up," you have just presented an argument. The first section states your conclusion, the second a reason for accepting the conclusion.

The Types of Reasoning

While authorities disagree as to the total number of major modes of reasoning, most agree that there are at least four. In this chapter let us examine these four basic modes of reasoning: Generalization, Analogy, Cause, and Sign. Understanding these forms of reasoning in order to use them correctly and to recognize them when they are used against an argument is essential to success in argumentative discourse. Just as you should be able to test evidence to be certain it is performing the task claimed for it, so should you be equally adept at testing the inferences drawn from the evidence to be certain they are correct.

Generalization

Generalizing, also called reasoning from example, is the process of inferring a conclusion about an entire group or classification from one or more specific cases or instances in point. This form of reasoning is frequently responsible for our attitudes, biases, and prejudices because we generalize about entire groups from a few personal experiences. Properly used, reasoning from examples can be an excellent means of proving an argument. The debater who quotes the Gallup Poll or reasons from statistics is usually drawing a generalization about something from a number of specific cases.

Generalizations should be tested to be certain they prove what is claimed. The crux of argument from example consists in presenting one or more individual instances of a certain class as fair specimens of a point and drawing an inference from them about the whole class. Three tests should be applied to this type of reasoning.

Test number one asks this: "Are the observed cases fair or typical examples?" It is not difficult to find examples to support any contention one wishes to make. Debaters have been known to falsify evidence; and students have been known to cheat on examinations; but are these typical examples? Gallup and Harris and other pollsters can accurately predict outcomes of national elections because the subjects polled are typical of those who will vote. The polls were so inaccurate in 1932 and again in 1948, because in 1932 the sample was not typical, and in 1948 the pollsters stopped polling too soon and did not sample the shift that took place in the last weeks prior to election day. So the examples must be checked for fairness.

The second test asks this question: "Have enough instances been examined to justify generalization?" Not only should the example used be fair or typical, but we should be certain there are enough samples to justify a generalization. Perhaps the major danger in arguing from example is drawing a conclusion from an insufficient number of instances, or making what is called a hasty generalization. The broader the classification to be tested, the larger the number of instances to be examined. Generalizing from the senior class in a high school and from the United States as a whole would certainly indicate a need for different size samples.

The third test asks: "Are there any negative instances?" It should never be forgotten that the other team has been analyzing the proposition and researching the evidence. What negative examples can they bring against the generalization? The wise debater always makes certain the generalization drawn is an accurate expression of what the sample has shown. One should not say *all* when the conclusions indicate at best *some, most,* or *seventy-five percent.* If you generalize too broadly from your examples, you lighten the burden of rebuttal your opponents have to carry.

Analogy

Argument from analogy asserts that if facts relating to A and facts relating to B are alike in certain known respects, they will be alike in other respects. Analogy is reasoning from the comparison of two cases. In one case a certain factor is known to exist, but in the other this same factor is under question. Whereas argument from generalization generalizes from one or more cases or examples, analogy infers a conclusion about one case by comparing it with another.

There are two types of analogy, literal and figurative. **Literal analogies** are those comparing like things from the same general class, such as man with man or cities with cities. The statement attributed to Patrick Henry, "Caesar had his Brutus, Charles the First his Cromwell, and George the Third may profit by their example," is a classic example of the literal analogy. Literal analogy is probably the more positive proof because it is literal. It compares like items. On the other hand, a figurative analogy can be more striking and gain quick belief with its attention-getting qualities. **Figurative analogies** are metaphorical, comparing two ideas or things of different classes, such as men and nations, men and ships, etc. Lincoln used a figurative analogy when he compared the dangers besetting the Union to Blonden, the tight rope walker, performing on his cable across Niagara Falls.

Arguments from analogy will involve at least two basic steps: first, pointing out the initial similarity of two or more things; and second, projecting the similarity to some new idea or conclusion. A fundamental test of any analogy is ascertaining if the points of essential likeness outweigh the points of essential difference. To do this, one seeks the answers to two questions about the analogy used: (1) Are the compared cases alike in all essential respects? (2) Are the differences in the compared cases accounted for?

Ronald Reagan frequently used simple audience related analogies to make a point. Fortunately for Reagan, there were times when most Americans seem to have accepted the analogy without scrutinizing it closely. For instance, when a suicide terrorist blew up an American embassy killing and injuring a number of the embassy staff, newspapers and TV newscasters blamed the White House for lax security measures, citing the fact that a large iron gate had not been put in place though it had been lying near the open gateway for some time awaiting somebody to get around to doing so, thus giving the terrorist easy access to the embassy. President Reagan denied that deficient security allowed the terrorist to get to the embassy, using this analogy: "About seventy-five percent of all the work that had to be done had been completed. Anybody that ever had their kitchen done over knows it never gets done as soon as you wish it would." Does this analogy really do what was demanded of it— deny that deficient security allowed the terrorist to get near the embassy? Are the compared cases alike in all essential respects? Are the differences in the compared cases accounted for? This was not some average American citizen's kitchen; this was an embassy of the United States. This was a job being done by people under the direct employment and supervision of the embassy. This was not a private citizen hiring an independent plumber who probably has several jobs going at the same time; works regular hours; is not faced with an emergency situation; and quite likely has the attitude if you do not like what he is doing, pay him and go find another plumber. Joe Citizen has very little to say as to when and how plumbers do the job. If this is how our embassies are protected in emergency situations, there would seem to be a deficiency in security. Incidentally, what type of analogy was Reagan using here— literal or figurative?

As a debater or as an individual, test the analogies you are exposed to. Make certain the analogies you use will pass the tests of being alike in all essential respects and being different in compared cases accounted for.

Causation

The third form of reasoning is causal argument. All causal arguments arise from the widely held belief that nothing happens without sufficient cause. In other words, a causal argument attempts to *account for or explain why* something is true. Simply defined, a causal argument asserts that if fact A exists, A will cause B to follow. This form of argument is used frequently in debates. Affirmatives use causal arguments to prove why certain problems exist. They use causal arguments to establish that if their plan is implemented, it will cause certain advantages. The negative frequently uses causal arguments to establish that if the affirmative's plan is implemented, it will cause certain disadvantages.

In preparing, attacking, or defending a causal argument, the debater should be familiar with essential tests of the validity of such arguments. These tests are based on the fact that any attack on causal reasoning is always directed toward the connection between cause and effect.

(1) *Is the cause capable of bringing about the effect? Or is there an unbroken relationship between the cause and the effect?*

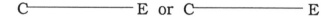

C———————— E or C———————— E

Superstitions are an example of faulty causal reasoning. It is difficult to show the unbroken relationship between, say, a broken mirror and seven years bad luck.

(2) *Will other causes intervene to prevent the cause-effect relationship?*

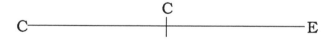

C
C————————+————————E

A historical example of not applying this test was the passage of the Eighteenth Amendment to prohibit the manufacture, transportation, and sale of alcoholic beverages for the purpose of ending the consumption of liquor in the United States. Causal factors intervened to nullify the desired effect. First of all, a great many Americans had no desire to quit drinking; secondly, anybody with the desire to do so could easily make wine or beer; and thirdly, the thirsty customers who were willing to pay a good price for a drink made bootlegging a profitable business. Failure to deal with attitudinal inherency defeated the case.

(3) *Is this the only cause that brings about the effect?* This is an important test and should not be neglected. It should be applied when arguing that a certain cause is the reason for the effect that sets up the need for change. The opposition may well argue that eliminating this particular cause will not solve the problem, because a number of causes have combined to produce the problem. Political office seekers and debaters are always looking for the simplified problem. Unfortunately, the propositions being debated by the office seekers and academic debaters are not simple problems. Inflation, world armaments, world trade, and unemployment (to name a few) are not simple cause-effect problems. In offering or attacking a causal argument, one of the indispensable tests is to ascertain if all the causes are included. *Is this the only cause?*

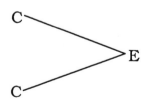

(4) *Is this the only effect?* When it is argued that

cutting taxes is beneficial because it puts more money in the taxpayers pocket, the cause-effect asserted may be true. *But are there other effects such as inflation or curtailed services?* In arguing that if a certain plan is put into effect certain good things will happen, the debater should be certain those are the only happenings or, if not the only happenings, be sure the advantages outweigh the disadvantages.

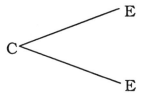

A causal argument is one that attempts to *account for* or *explain why* something is true. It does not try to establish that the proposition is true, but *assuming its truth*, attempts to show what causes it to be true.

Sign

An argument from sign is the fourth and final mode of reasoning to be discussed here. Arguments from sign are derived from the assumption that certain facts will always or usually accompany each other. As a result, the presence of one will be an indication of the presence of the other. Arguments from sign are based on the generalization that all cases of A are indications of B. Sign reasoning is argument which indicates that something *is* true without attempting to explain *why* it is true.

We frequently reason from sign. One day on campus a young man meets an attractive young woman, then notices she is wearing a fraternity pin. He concludes that she is going steady. State Department officials notice that a prominent Chinese leader no longer attends party functions and that he is in party disfavor. The young man has not reasoned why the young woman is going steady, just that she is. The State Department may have no clue as to why the Chinese party leader is in trouble; they just feel certain that he is.

Because sign reasoning is obviously based upon generalizations previously formed, the validity of any argument from sign depends on the reliability of the generalization as well as the soundness of the signs. Therefore, the debater must be certain the generalization is valid. The signs may be examined by answering the following questions:

(1) *Is the sign relationship accidental or coincidental?* Maybe the young lady borrowed a friend's sweater and did not notice the pin. Perhaps the Chinese leader is ill, but government officials do not want to announce this fact.

(2) *Have special factors intervened to alter the sign?* Many years ago a college negative team was having a very successful season arguing that diplomatic recognition should not be extended to Soviet Russia, because the language

of the Soviet constitution called for world revolution and denial of human rights. An affirmative team countered this sign reasoning with a then recently adopted new constitution that did not call for world revolution and guaranteed rights previously denied. Among other things, the negative team learned the value of keeping up to date on research.

(3) *Is the sign reliable without the collaboration or concurrence of other signs?* Circumstantial evidence in the law is sign reasoning, but to gain belief beyond a reasonable doubt usually requires the presence of several signs. Bruno Hauptman was convicted and executed for the kidnapping and death of the Charles Lindbergh baby because he possessed the ransom money; he was a carpenter; he had an accent matching that of the man who collected the ransom money; and because the ladder used in the kidnapping had been built with wood matching wood stored in Hauptman's house.

Thus any reasoning from sign must be tested to make sure that both the generalization upon which it is based and the signs themselves are reliable.

Faulty reasoning is usually the result of ignorance on the part of the debater. Many individuals simply do not understand how to reason from example, analogy, cause, or sign. To argue effectively the debater must have a good working knowledge of the evidence available and be skilled and practiced in the use of the various modes of reasoning.

7
CHAPTER

Debating the Affirmative

The Theory

In traditional debate theory, the prime responsibility of the affirmative was the advocacy of the proposition; it was their duty to win all the issues in the debate, thereby gaining acceptance of both their case and plan. During the 1970's this view changed somewhat; affirmatives offered their particular plan as an example of the resolution and argued specifically for its adoption. Nevertheless, most affirmatives of that era, if pressed, would admit that the resolution was the ultimate ground which they were defending. Today, especially on the collegiate level, the proposition itself is almost ignored and most affirmatives argue only for the adoption of their specific plan as a desirable policy alternative.   Whether you, as an affirmative, advocate the proposition or only your own particular plan; you operate in the debate with a number of duties, responsibilities, and advantages.

Basic Concepts

• Definitions

It is both the responsibility and the privilege of the affirmative to define the terms of the resolution. As long as the definition you present is reasonable, it should serve as the basis for the debate. Even if the negative presents an equally reasonable series of meanings, the affirmative interpretation should stand unless it is shown to be illegitimate.

In defining terms you should use both restraint and common sense. As we remarked in Chapter Three, the words of the topic, if defined individually, will often give a terribly skewed meaning to the proposition. If there is a basic or specialized meaning to a phrase used in the resolution, reason dictates that it is the phrase and not its component words which should be defined. There are many terms in each resolution, such as the ubiquitous "should", which need no definition. Sometimes, however, there are words not appearing in the proposition which will become crucial as the case unfolds; for clarity, these might need to be defined at the start of the presentation.

There are two major methods of definition: **denotative** and **operational**. The former takes the meaning straight from the dictionary and defines the words or phrases in terms of other words or phrases. The operational approach is definition by example; the most common way of doing this is to present the affirmative plan as one example of what the resolution might mean. Whichever method you choose, the affirmative has the task of making sure the debate proceeds on common ground.

• Harm

The affirmative must next show that a problem exists in the present system. This may take the form of a serious evil; a widespread difficulty; the failure to obtain a desirable advantage; an incorrect or awkward procedure; or any of numerous other directions. Whatever form the problem takes, the argument is basically the same: We have today a less than optimum situation which should and can be corrected. The harm may take either of two general forms— quantitative or qualitative. In the former instance you claim a specific identifiable loss, either loss of money, of lives, of productivity, or of some commodity. Many judges and most negatives are quick to demand this type of numerical harm from an affirmative team. A qualitative harm, on the other hand, usually defies reduction to figures but may be just as important. Examples of this might be a loss of freedom, a decline in the respect for the law, or some damage of similar ilk. The establishment of such a harm usually depends on opinion evidence from experts and is likely to prove more of a burden to the affirmative than quantification. Whatever form is employed, however, it is the duty of the affirmative to establish a harm.

• Significance

Thirdly, the affirmative must show that their harm is significant. The loss of a few thousand dollars or a few lives, as deplorable as that might be, is usually not sufficient reason to change an entire system. If the figures rise to millions of dollars and scores of lives, the picture certainly changes in the affirmative's favor. If it is billions of dollars and hundreds of lives, the significance seems virtually unquestionable. Exactly how much significance is enough is impossible to state, since it will vary from debate to debate and is always an arguable issue in the round. Traditionally the affirmative attempted to establish as much significance as possible. In the new approach to debate common on the collegiate level in the 1980's, teams often deliberately minimize their significance to lessen the impact of any negative disadvantages; this concept will be more thoroughly discussed in Chapter Thirteen.

• Inherency

The next affirmative burden is your most difficult and is probably the most complex issue in the whole field of argumentation; this is inherency.[1] Inherency may be defined as the ability of the present system, extended to its logical limits, to solve the problem which the affirmative has identified. If the status quo can deal with the difficulty, then we should not change, since it would be a waste of time and resources to institute a new scheme to do that which we are already capable of doing. Only if the present system is found wanting should we consider altering it.

There are three major forms which inherency may take. The first of these is **gap** inherency. Here no structure, agency, law, or decision of any type exists to take care of the problem; there is truly a gap in the status quo's organization. If you claim this type of inherency, you should carefully study the laws dealing with the issue and investigate all agencies which might have jurisdiction over the matter. Only when you can satisfy yourself, and more importantly the judge, that nobody can do anything about the problem, will this inherency stand.

The second, and most traditional form of inherency is **structural**. Here a law, court decision, or administrative regulation actually prohibits doing what the affirmative claims is necessary to solve the problem. If, for example, the affirmative wanted to solve poverty by simply giving money to all the poor, they would quickly discover that the law requires people to be more than poor in order to get help. They must be blind, disabled, elderly, or in some other accepted category (the so-called categorical approach to welfare); and many of our poor fit in no such category. Thus the very structure of the system would prevent this solution to the problem, and the affirmative would need to make an inherent change in order to implement their plan. It should be noted that simple lack of money or manpower is not a sufficient inherency argument. If the structure exists, the lack of funds or personnel will not be solved by creating a new agency. The structure itself must be at fault in order for inherency to be established.

The third type of inherency, the most difficult to work with, has become the most popular form; this is **attitudinal** inherency. Here the affirmative argues that the attitudes or opinions of those in power are so fixed in favor of the *status quo* that the problem will never be solved unless these individuals can be removed or circumvented. A good example is the registration of blacks in the South during the 1960's. Those in charge of registration on the local level were so opposed to the integrated voting booth that they used every possible device to discourage the would-be voters. The federal government finally stepped in, solving the problem by sending federal registrars to some areas and passing laws which forbade the use of repressive devices. The attitudes in this case were not changed, but simply circumvented and thus rendered powerless.

The major difficulty with attitudinal inherency is finding a proper way to get around the attitudes. If they exist at a lower level of government, as in the above example, it is easy to remove authority to the federal level; but what does one do when the destructive attitudes are at the highest levels of authority? This difficulty was one of the major reasons for the proliferation in affirmative plans during the 1970's of "independent, five-member, self-perpetuating, munificently-salaried boards" to oversee the solution to the problem. Only such an agency seems capable of getting around the attitudinal blocks at the centers of power. Attitudinal inherency may be the most difficult type to employ, but it may well be the most realistic. As one coach has observed, "Since attitudes are the reasons we pass laws and decide court cases, perhaps all inherency is, at base, attitudinal."

• Solvency

The word "solvency" appeared on the forensic scene in the 1970's. It replaced, but means virtually the same as plan-meets-need, and has the advantage of being a less cumbersome term. It is the requirement of the affirmative to show that their plan will solve the problem they have isolated. This may be done by analogy with some locality which has tried a similar program or through testimony of experts giving their best judgment of the worth of this new approach.

• Topicality

It is the responsibility of the affirmative to present a case which falls reasonably within the bounds of the proposition. While this might seem self-evident, numerous teams each season present cases which, at least on the surface, have little or nothing to do with the topic. Sometimes the mistake is an innocent and honest one, the affirmative having discovered a different slant than the rest of the debate community. All too often, however, it is the deliberate attempt of a team to put one over on the opposition by presenting a trick case for which the negative will be unprepared. Trick cases or semantic interpretations of the resolution do sometimes win, but some judges vote them down out of hand. They are usually good only for the first tournament against unprepared teams, and they tend to give an unsavory reputation to the teams who consistently use them. Each affirmative should attempt to remain within the bounds of a reasonably defined proposition.

• Extratopicality

It is further the responsibility of the affirmative to be certain that their solution to the problem flows directly from the resolution. As will be discussed below, as long as a plan implements the resolution, it may do as many other things as it wishes; the solution to the problem, however, must come from those plan planks which implement the proposition, not from any other extraneous provision. If the solution comes from some non-resolutional plank of the plan, that clearly indicates that the proposition is not needed to solve the problem and the affirmative loses.

• Justification

Some judges and debaters insist that it is the responsibility of the affirmative, as the appointed defenders of the proposition, to justify every important term in the resolution. For example, you must be prepared to show, upon a mere challenge, "Why the federal government?" if the federal level is specified in the proposition. This is a minority position, however, with many judges requiring the negative to present some substantive objection before demanding proof of the affirmative. The wise advocate, however, is ready for the justification judges and has defenses of important terms prepared beforehand.

• Fiat

Fiat is the right of the affirmative to assume, for purposes of argument, the adoption of their plan. The word "should" as employed in propositions of policy is traditionally defined as "ought to, but not necessarily will be." Further interpreted, this means that your obligation is limited to showing that the adoption of the resolution would be a good thing; you are not required to show that any legislative body actually would adopt it. Indeed, showing that a legislature would so act might be construed as a serious inherency defect in the affirmative's case. Fiat is sometimes referred to as the "golden moment" in which time and belief are suspended; before the moment is the present system and after it is the affirmative plan. Negatives who try to argue that no one would actually pass such a law as the affirmative has proposed are guilty of what is known as a should/would argument— that is, they are trying to hold the affirmative to a greater burden than the rules of the activity impose. In such an instance, you need only point out what the negative is doing in order to defeat the argument.

The benefit of fiat is not, however, a legitimate answer to circumvention plan attacks. If the negative is able to show that plan opponents will cripple the plan after it goes into effect, that stands as a reason not to adopt it in the first place. Fiat is proof only against the above-mentioned should/would argument.

Organizational Patterns

There are four organizational patterns which you may use in the development of your affirmative case. The first of these is the traditional or **need-plan case**. When using this approach you begin with the present system and find within it a serious evil which cannot be corrected without changing the entire system. You then construct a plan to deal with the problem. This type of case is best employed when the present system is in serious difficulty, and the evil that it causes is evident.

The second pattern has become by far the most popular case form; this is the **comparative advantages approach**. Here you should begin by constructing a plan which beneficially alters the existing system; the advantages flowing from such a plan are then developed. These advantages must be proved unique to the particular plan the affirmative has presented; this, of course, is a fulfilling of the inherency requirement. The comparative advantages approach is most often used when the present system cannot be shown to be positively evil. In almost any structure, however, changes can always be made for the better, and the comparative advantages approach makes use of that fact.

Thirdly, you may employ a **goals case**. With such an approach you choose a desirable end and then develop a means to achieve that end. The particular goal you select may be either pre-existent or created. The **pre-existent goal** is one which society already espouses, but has not been able to achieve, such as full employment, the elimination of poverty, etc. A **created goal** is one originated by the affirmative team. A pre-existent goal is usually stronger since the negative cannot attack it without abandoning at least part of the present system's philosophy. In developing the goals approach you should also be prepared to show that your plan is the most desirable way of achieving the ultimate end.

Finally, you may employ a **criteria case**. This approach works from a perspective opposite that of the goals case. With the criteria type of development you discover the characteristics of the best solution to a particular problem and argue that a plan which meets these criteria is superior to any other method. Thus, when the colleges were debating the question of poverty several years ago, one team set up such criteria as cash payments, payments to all the poor, payments on an annual basis, etc., and argued that their approach, which employed all of these, was the best way to proceed.

It should be emphasized that whatever approach is used, the basic requirements remain the same. You must show a difficulty that is significant and inherent and must present a plan which works successfully to solve the problem.

The Practical Approach

• Developing the Affirmative Case

The debater, unlike the sports competitor, almost never enjoys a physical home court advantage. Most of the tournaments you attend are at other schools; and even if your institution hosts a tournament, you are often not allowed to enter competitively. Nevertheless, a home court advantage of another type does exist for the debater; it is your affirmative case. For most participants in the activity, one half of all contests will be on the affirmative, and it thus behooves you to approach with great care the choice and construction of your affirmative case.

The question of which affirmative to use at the start of the season is a major policy decision. If you wait until the last minute and then pick what seems easiest to get ready in a short period of time, you are throwing away one of your best advantages. Instead, the process should begin considerably before the first tournament with careful weighing of the alternatives, consideration of the available evidence, and finally a choice of the best approach.

Many debaters are constant case switchers, changing their affirmatives almost every week in the hope of surprising their opposition. For the most part such individuals achieve far less than they would if they selected carefully at the beginning and then tried to enhance and develop their material throughout the season. Since the affirmative case is the debaters' home ground, they should know more about it than any possible opponent; such knowledge will always elude the constant switcher.

On occasion it does become necessary to change one's case during the season. Perhaps it gets enacted into law (this has actually happened to some teams); possibly a significant number of judges are simply refusing to accept the approach as topical; or negatives have come up with that unbeatable disadvantage which just had not been considered. For whatever reason, if the case needs to be changed, it is better to do it than to suffer through with a losing position. Insofar as possible, when selecting a replacement case, go through the same extensive process employed in the choice of the original affirmative. A word of pessimism is necessary at this point: teams which are forced to change their cases in mid-season usually, although admittedly not always, do not do as well as those who hit on the "right" approach at the start.

In writing the affirmative, it is usually best to begin with the plan, since that is the area of greatest concern in today's debates. A plan has two major functions: to enact the resolution and to avoid disadvantages. Both these objectives are achieved through a series of **planks** which together comprise the completed plan. The first step should be the composition of a plan plank which enacts the resolution; from this should flow all the advantages which will be claimed (see the comments above concerning extratopicality). Next, you should consider all the related concepts, functions, and aids which would be necessary to the operation of such a policy option. The plan will need administration, oversight, staff, information, funding, penalties for violation, enforcement, etc.; all of these should be provided. How will the plan work? A brief description of the duties the proposal involves is usually necessary. When you have completed a list of all you think needs to be in the plan, you should condense it to the most concise language possible; organize it logically into its component planks; and set it aside for the moment.

Next, give attention to the case side. Here you will need to decide what harms the plan solves or what advantages you will claim from it. The building blocks of the case are called contentions; they are much like the major headings one finds in a public speech. Their exact number may differ from case to case but generally there are between two and five of them in the first affirmative. Sometimes in a multiple advantage case each contention is a separate advantage; in other cases there may be only one advantage, built from several contentions. Determine the appropriate organizational pattern and number of contentions. Once this is done, the case should be outlined. This will insure that all the parts are properly subordinated and that the whole structure hangs together logically. Once the outline seems satisfactory, you should flesh it out by putting the material in a more narrative form. With both the case and plan in reasonable shape, it is time to start thinking about the defense of your approach in light of possible negative attacks.

The best way to prepare for opposition arguments is to put yourself temporarily in the shoes of a negative meeting your case and develop all the arguments of which you can think. You should begin with the plan, construct every objection imaginable, and then set out to provide the necessary answers. Some arguments may be answered by the logic of the plan itself; others may be solved by the addition of a plan spike; and some may require independent responses. A **plan spike** is an additional plank whose sole purpose is to negate a possible objection. It is a perfectly legitimate addition to the plan as long as no advantage is claimed from it. If an advantage flows from the spike, however, that advantage would be extra-topical. Whatever type of answer you employ against plan objections, all of its ramifications and implications should be understood; the logic of the argument must be carried out to the last rebuttal extension to make certain that you have discovered the best response available.

You then return to the case and perform the same brainstorming process there. Some arguments may be answered by rewording or reorganizing the contentions; some will require new extensions. Once again, the ultimate logic of the position taken must be considered, even when that position has to be extended in each of the remaining affirmative speeches. All this preparation may seem like a great deal of trouble, but it can save the even greater difficulty which arises from running into an argument for which you are totally unprepared.

With the ideas thoroughly thought out you may now give a little elegance to the speech. The first affirmative constructive is practically the only speech in the debate which can be prepared beforehand; thus, careful stylistic devices are an element from which it alone can benefit. Variations in style, careful transitions between contentions, a catchy introduction, and a strong conclusion will all enhance any speech. When all this has been done, you will have a case of which you can be proud and on which you can depend in those crucial rounds which, hopefully, you will contest during the year.

• Affirmative Presentations

After the first affirmative has been presented and has been responded to by the first negative, it then becomes the duty of the second affirmative constructive to restore the arguments to their initial strength or even beyond. The most important task of the 2AC is coverage. Any items which are neglected in this speech are probably lost, since there simply is not time to handle them anew in the rebuttals. Additionally, many judges will discount arguments dropped in the constructive which a team tries to resuscitate in the rebuttals.

There are several techniques which the second speaker can use in covering of all the important material. First, during practice rounds you should note the length of time it takes to cover a particular amount of material. Then, using the signals from the timekeeper as clues, you can judge rather accurately whether to dawdle over an argument or whether to fly from that point on to get in all the material. Secondly, the use of prepared blocks can make a great difference in the effectiveness of the coverage. Having worked out ahead of time as many of the possible opposition arguments as you can, you should write out your responses, complete with evidence and transitions, on sheets of paper. These may be filed in a loose-leaf binder and taken out for use in the round. Then, when the particular argument to which the block responds is presented, you will have a ready-made answer which is carefully thought out and there for the using. Often a block will contain several lines of response, and if pressed for time you can omit some of the less important replies. If the second affirmative can so devastate the case attacks that the negative has trouble extending, the debate is in excellent shape.

The first affirmative rebuttal has been accurately called the most crucial speech in the debate. Seldom can a debate be won by this speech alone, but almost always it can be lost there, either by unsatisfactory answers or by poor coverage of ground.   The 1AR should invariably begin with the plan objections since those stand without answer at that point in the debate; you should then return to the case, covering as many of the crucial points as you have time for. It is imperative, however, that all of the P. O.'s receive some kind of answer. If, through accident or design, the 1AR fails to respond to a significant objection, most judges will opt for the negative on the spot.

The time division within the first affirmative rebuttal is a question of some importance. For many years speakers would spend much of their time on the plan.   Later it became the fashion to divide the speech as evenly as possible, spending at least two minutes back on the case. Today, with the stronger second affirmative constructives and weaker first negative rebuttals, 1AR has reverted to a slighting of the case, with many speakers spending a minute or less there. Exactly how the time is divided is a decision for the particular team and may well vary from round to round. However it is handled, the time division should be a conscious decision and not one simply forced on the affirmative during an unplanned presentation.

There are several devices the first rebuttalist may use to save precious time. As with your colleague in the constructive, having carefully thought out ahead of time answers to all the conceivable objections, you should block them out for ease and speed of presentation. This is probably the most useful technique available. Secondly, arguments may be lumped together. Perhaps two arguments will rest on the same premise. Time should not be wasted answering them both; lump them. As a general rule, use the quickest or easiest answer available; this will, at least, throw the burden back on the last negative to force him to make a response in order to carry the argument. For example, if an argument is missing a crucial link, such as a motive for circumvention or uniqueness of a disadvantage, the negative should have to provide such before the affirmative launches into a long response to this material. If a plan-meet-advantage argument is in contradiction with an inherency argument, the affirmative should point it out and make the negative either explain the discrepancy or drop one of the positions. While this technique does have the possible disadvantage of allowing a trap in the last negative rebuttal, the quick answer is still usually preferable. Many negatives are not trying to be clever; they simply lack the links they have failed to provide. Responding briefly will, more often than not, prove the most advantageous approach for you in the first affirmative rebuttal.

The last affirmative speech also carries a heavy burden, since it is the final opportunity to win the debate for your side. It is generally agreed that you should begin with the plan objections, since they will often need a lot of work, and then return to the case, finishing the debate on your home ground. Time allocation can be a problem here, too; you must make certain not to overkill on the objections, leaving too little time available for the case.

The final rebuttalist must be able to synthesize the debate, showing how each of the original issues has come through relatively unscathed and how a particular response has won each of them for the affirmative. The coverage of ground must be specific, and yet the overall philosophy of the affirmative must not be lost in the welter of tiny subpoints, as decisive as those may be. In essence, the last rebuttal specifically summarizes the debate from the affirmative point of view.

• Affirmative Strategies

Several general strategic devices are available to the affirmative. One of the most elementary of these is the decision between the use of a unified or multiple independent case. In the unified case you claim only one advantage or harm; in a manner of speaking, you place all your eggs in one basket. In the multiple case you develop two or more independent advantages, each within itself a sufficient reason to adopt the resolution. Each approach has its benefits and defects. The unified case allows more time for development so that a really strong position may be established. Of course, if one element of it, such as significance or inherency, is defeated, then the debate is lost. The multiple approach, on the other hand, does not allow nearly as much time for initial development and puts a greater burden on later speakers to cover the ground established. It does protect against a weakness in one of the advantages since, in a three-part case two of the advantages may be lost, but if the third one carries intact, the debate may still be won. This also allows you to pick and choose late in the debate whether to try to win or to drop one or more of the advantages. You must decide which of these approaches to use on the basis of the strength your arguments have and on your own skills as debaters.

You may choose to sandbag an argument. **Sandbagging** is delaying presentation of the substance of an argument until a later point in the debate. Since no new arguments may be presented in rebuttals and there is not time there to develop new material anyway, this means withholding some material until the second affirmative constructive. Reasons for doing this may vary; it may be done for purposes of surprise, to waste the time of the first negative, or to prevent having to extend a weak argument a third time. For example, quantification of significance might be withheld until the negative demands its presentation. This means that their first opportunity for substantive reply will be in the first negative rebuttal. There must be a good strategic reason for using this device, since some judges frown on this technique, especially where *prima facie* elements of the case are involved.

One interesting technique which may be used to take advantage of the specific talents of debaters is reversal of speaking order in the affirmative rebuttals. Here one speaker takes the first and last speeches in the debate, and the other gives both the 2AC and the 1AR. The major reason for doing this should be the contrasting styles of the debaters. If one is more skilled as a speaker and has good analytical and persuasive skills, that person would be better in the outsides; if the other is more of a technician and is faster, then that debater should take the insides. Once again, this technique should not be used just for the sake of using it; you should employ it only if it fits the situation. The judge and the opponents should be notified before the round if you intend to switch rebuttals.

A strategic type of case organization which may be successful in certain instances is the **modular approach**. Sometimes a plan will produce a large number of advantages, many more than can be presented in one eight or ten minute speech. In such a situation the various advantages may be treated as modules which can be plugged into or taken out of the presentation depending on the situation in the particular round. If a team has heard some of the advantages before, it might be well to surprise them with new ones; if a judge does not like certain arguments, present others. If this approach is used, each modular advantage should be carefully timed so that the speech can be fitted into the minutes available. In addition, the transitions should be rather neutral in phrasing so that they will carry the speaker without difficulty from one advantage into the next.

Finally, the late 1970's saw the emer-

gence on the college level of a quite revolutionary approach to debating the affirmative; this is
the **alternative justification** case. Briefly
stated, it contains not only independent advantages, which may be defended or dropped as the
affirmative desires, but also independent plans
which may be similarly treated. Thus, an affirmative might offer three separate examples of
the resolution with an advantage or two coming
from each one; all they would need to do, in the
view of those supporting this approach, is to win
one of the plans and one of the advantages
flowing from it in order to carry the debate. This
type of case has found favor with a number of
teams, but with many fewer judges. While it is
certainly an interesting innovation, in both a
philosophic and a strategic sense it carries with
it several problems.

On the philosophic level, alternative justification violates the strict policy option debate
situation, since the judge must now consider
not just the negative policy versus the affirmative, but the negative versus several affirmatives. This is simply too much to hope to
accomplish with any depth in the limited time
available to the participants. Secondly, it is
critical to remember that the ultimate duty of
the affirmative is not the advocacy of a specific
case, but through their case the advocacy of the
resolution. Since each of the affirmative plans
must, in order to be topical, be a legitimate
interpretation of the proposition, if the judge
votes for the affirmative he or she is, of necessity, voting for all the plans, whether the affirmative has ceased to defend them or not. This

means that the judge may well be voting for two bad policies along with one good one. For example, if one plan has been dropped because of a terrible disadvantage and another is worthless because an absolute plan-meet-advantage argument has eliminated all its advantages and the judge votes for the third plan because it carries intact, he or she still gets as unwanted baggage plans one and two, complete with disadvantage and uselessness. This argument alone would seem to cast serious doubt on the alternative justification approach. Finally, game theorists usually reject this case form on the grounds that it violates the balance of play by placing too great a burden on the negative. In spite of these objections, if an affirmative wishes to attempt such a case, judges should be chosen with the utmost caution.[2]

As previously argued, the choice of a strong affirmative case is one of the most important considerations you have; and wise decisions there may pay dividends far above those available from expending equal amounts of time on other aspects of the activity. If your case is strong and is able to win the majority of the debates in which you use it, a successful season is highly likely.

NOTES

1. For an interesting look at the issue of inherency, see Tom Goodnight, Bill Balthrop and Donn W. Parson, "The Problem of Inherency: Strategy and Substance," *Journal of the American Forensic Association*, X, 4 (Spring, 1974), pp. 229-240.

2. For pro and con views of alternative justification see Allan Lichtman, Charles Garvin, and Jerry Corsi, "The Alternative-Justification Affirmative: A New Case Form," *Journal of the American Forensic Association*, X, 2 (Fall, 1973), pp. 59-69; and Robert V. Seltzer, "The Alternative-Justification Affirmative: Practical and Theoretical Implications," *Journal of the American Forensic Association*, XI, 3 (Winter, 1975), pp. 131-136.

8

Debating the Negative

The Theory

The duty of the negative in a policy debate is to win one or more of the issues in the round, thus defeating the opposition or the plan. Such an issue may be either substantive or technical. A substantive issue is one actually raised by or against the particular affirmative case approach; it is an item such as inherency, significance, or a plan attack. Technical issues, on the other hand, discuss the relation of the affirmative case to the topic and include topicality, extra-topicality, and justification. These technical arguments may be just as important as the substantive ones and should always be raised if there is any doubt at all about the legitimacy of the affirmative case. If technical arguments are used, they should be presented early in the first negative constructive and then extended throughout the round as would be done with any other issue. Given the disposition of most judges and the nature of most debates, it is probably unwise to depend solely on technical arguments to win a decision.

Just as there are two parts to the affirmative presentation (case and plan), there are two parts to the negative attack. The first negative constructive dealt traditionally with the opposition's case and the second constructive with the affirmative plan.

• First Negative Approaches

There are, generally speaking, four major options open to the first negative in attacking the case. The first of these is **direct refutation**. In this approach you stand for nothing in particular and defend no specific ground, but merely attack the affirmative presentation. You are, by implication, resting on the *status quo*; since if you are victorious and the proposition is rejected, the *status quo* is what would be left; you specifically refrain from a defense of the present system. This option has some philosophical weaknesses and may cause the judge to wonder what is wrong with the *status quo*, since you refuse to rest openly upon it. In addition, a strong policy option judge may regard this approach as extremely poor since it provides no policy to compare with the affirmative's.

The second approach is a direct **defense of the *status quo*.** Here you openly announce your stand; argue that the present system is working as well as can be expected; and claim that it is solving the problem on its own. This gives a more solid basis for attack on the affirmative and allows the judge an option with which to compare the affirmative plan.

The third approach, and by far the most common and realistic, is the ***status quo* with repairs.** It is generally true that an existing structure is far from perfect. Indeed, the very fact that this subject has been chosen for debate strongly implies that someone thinks something is presently wrong. This particular stand of the negative admits that all is not as it might be but denies that the total structure is hopeless. It argues that with a few judicious corrections here and there what we have will serve very well. The major danger in this approach is that the repairs needed may turn out to be so extensive that we would do better to scrap the whole thing and start anew. In some debates negatives have become so carried away with this approach that they have proposed changes far more structural and sweeping than those of the affirmative. You must remember that inherency is bounded by the logical extremes of the current structures. If repairs stay short of that line, then the negative is probably on safe ground.

The final major option open to you is the **counterplan**. This is the most radical of all negative approaches; this device is not recommended for beginners. The counterplan is best used when the *status quo* appears to be hopeless. The affirmative has found overwhelming weaknesses in it, or you realize that it is beyond saving. In order to defeat the proposition, therefore, you abandon the *status quo* and advocate yet a third option— something not resolutional, but not the present system either. A counterplan is usually framed like an affirmative plan, with sufficient planks and mechanisms to do the job needed.

There are several rules dealing with the counterplan; while not all judges agree with the ideas set forth here, most of the knowledgeable experts in the field would concur with them. First, the counterplan must not be topical. Some negatives have taken their own affirmative case and tried to use it as a counterplan; with competent judges they have always lost (unless, of course, their own case was untopical, which gave them a problem of a different sort). The reason for this rule is simple: it is the business of the affirmative to advocate the resolution and that of the negative to oppose it. If the negative advocates an approach which is resolutional, the negative is in essence agreeing with the affirmative that the proposition should be adopted. In such a case, the affirmative should win.

Secondly, the counterplan must be competitive, *i.e.*, it must solve the affirmative harm or accrue the affirmative advantages. If it does not do so, or does not do so as well as the affirmative plan, then it is an inferior policy option; and again the affirmative should win.

Finally, the negative counterplan should offer additional advantages, thus making it in some way superior to the affirmative approach. It is generally wise to have these additional advantages in the same area as the topic; i.e., if the topic is medical care, then the advantage should have something to do with medicine. Some judges do not require this similarity; after all, if the counterplan is non-topical, why could not an advantage coming from it deal with anything? This reasoning seems to make sense, but since it is a minority position, the counterplan user should probably supply advantages in the general topical area. It should be added that some judges believe that a counterplan must have additional advantages to win. This would seem to be unnecessary, since it is the duty of the affirmative to advocate the resolution as the best approach; if the negative counterplan alone is as good as the affirmative plan, then the affirmative is not the best and should lose. Nevertheless, this too is a minority position, and additional advantages are a wise precaution whenever counterplanning.

Thus, with a choice of at least four available options, the first negative should be able to advance strong, meaningful attacks against the affirmative case.

• Second Negative Approaches

The second negative has four lines of argument to launch against the affirmative plan; the first of these is **workability**. A workability argument is leveled against the mechanism of the plan itself and contends that something within the plan's own structure will prevent it from operating properly. Like a piece of machinery with one of its cogs misaligned, the plan will fail to function or simply collapse of its own inherent defects. Perhaps the affirmative has forgotten to provide any enforcement against violators of their plan; perhaps they have neglected to provide compensation for their administrators; or possibly there is no provision for adequate and necessary information. Whatever defect is discovered, workability is usually an absolute voting issue, since the plan can hardly produce any beneficial effects if it simply self-destructs when put into operation.

The second type of plan objection is the **plan-meet-need** or **plan-meet-advantage** argument (commonly abbreviated PMN or PMA). This argument maintains that the plan will not solve the problem it has been designed to correct. You may claim, first of all, that the difficulty simply defies solution and that nothing can correct it. This approach should be used cautiously since it will, of course, contradict any inherency arguments used in the first negative speech. Far more common is the contention that some additional force which the affirmative has not considered will interfere with the plan's achieving its goal. When the colleges were debating the question of poverty, many affirmatives would give the poor a cash income based on the Social Security poverty line. This is only a subsistence level, however, and is sufficient only if every dollar is well spent. Negatives would argue that many of the poor did not know how to budget their income and had bad buying habits; thus they would misspend their new income and the problem of poverty, which the affirmative was trying to solve, would still exist. By failing to take into account the additional factor of education, the affirmative had constructed a plan which did not meet their need.

PMA's may be partial or absolute in nature. Partial PMA's, as with the example above, detract from the affirmative advantage but do not totally eliminate it. The judge must then weigh how much advantage is left against other negative arguments. An absolute PMA, on the other hand, completely destroys the advantage, preventing the plan from achieving anything. This is the type of argument for which you should search.

Finally, a PMA does not have to be unique to the affirmative plan. If some element prevents both the plan and the present system from working, the fact that the present system cannot solve the difficulty is irrelevant; if the plan cannot achieve a solution, it should not be adopted. To use an example from the colleges' energy topic of a few years ago, a plan calling for increased use of deep-mined coal might face a

PMA argument that because there are insufficiently trained miners we could not increase production. A first affirmative rebuttal response that this applies also to the present system (and thus to the negative inherency arguments) would be true but irrelevant. If the plan cannot meet the need it should not be adopted, no matter what other facts are true.

The third type of plan objection is the **circumvention** argument. This position contends that some group of individuals desires to maintain the *status quo* and wishes to prevent the plan from working; this argument is especially potent when the affirmative has based its inherency on attitudes. In order for the circumvention argument to be established, two items must be proved: motive and mechanism. If the affirmative has used attitudinal inherency, the **motive** is already established. If not, you must prove that someone dislikes the provisions of the plan so strongly that they would risk whatever penalties it provides in order to try to disrupt its operations. Secondly, you must prove the existence of a **mechanism** through which the opponents of the plan can work their evil. It does even the most adamant of opponents little good if there is no way in which they can effectively act. As with an old-fashioned murder mystery, the "killer" must have both reason and opportunity to do the dastardly deed.

The final type of plan objection— to many the most important— is the **disadvantage**. This objection agrees that the plan will work; indeed, it depends on the plan's being put into operation. The disadvantage (often abbreviated DA) argues that the plan will produce some disastrous consequence, unforeseen by the affirmative, which will render conditions worse than they were before it went into effect. For example, if the affirmative were advocating a plan calling for pollution control and proposed to install control equipment on all factories, you might raise a disadvantage dealing with unemployment or one claiming vastly increased prices leading to inflation; either of these situations could be argued as being worse than the original problem which the affirmative had hoped to solve.

The disadvantage needs to be constructed much like the contentions of an affirmative case. First, the harmful nature of the disadvantage must be shown. Next, the significance of this harm must be proved; an insignificant disadvantage, like an insignificant advantage to an affirmative case, achieves little. Finally, the disadvantage must be shown to be inherent, that is unique, to the affirmative plan. The reason for this requirement is clear. If the disadvantage exists both in the present system and under the plan, both suffer from the evil. In such a case the advantages flowing from the plan would give good reason to adopt it; only if the plan produces a unique disadvantage should the affirmative stance be rejected. A disadvantage may claim that the plan produces a brand new problem or that it greatly magnifies an existing one.

The Practical Approach

    As a practical matter, the old rule concerning the negative's need to win only one of the issues in order to win the debate does not always hold true today. It depends in part on which issue is won and to a larger extent on the judge and his biases. Most judges will give the negative the debate if they win inherency or a significant disadvantage. Many fewer would award the debate solely on a plan-meet-advantage, and a number might give a win to an affirmative which has only miniscule significance if the negative has no outstanding disadvantages. It is, therefore, to your advantage to concentrate your arguments in those areas which judges consider important.

    The majority of today's judges consider themselves **policy option** decision makers. In this view, they are legislators deciding whether or not to pass a bill. They are being asked to decide between two options: the affirmative plan and the negative stance, whatever that may be. It is to your advantage to have a clearly stated position which you may offer to counter the affirmative's approach. Wise negatives begin their first constructive with a statement of philosophy; this allows them to refer back to their original stand during the debate. It gives the judge a policy for which to vote.

    In keeping with the policy option philosophy, most judges demand of the negative a consistent position. They will not allow the first negative to take one stand and the second to adopt a contradictory pose. If discrepancies appear, the affirmative need only point out the inconsistency in order to have the judge disallow both arguments until the negative is able to explain away the contradiction or until they drop one of the positions. This type of inconsistency is most likely to arise between an inherency attack and a plan-meet-advantage attack. If there is a reason why the plan will not work, it is often quite likely that the same problems also function in the *status quo* to keep it from working as well. In this case you must be prepared to explain clearly why the positions are not inconsistent. Sometimes they are so obviously in conflict that one speaker or the other must sacrifice an argument to the greater good of the team effort. Return, for instance, to the previously used example of coal mines and insufficient miners. If the first negative's inherency attacks had argued that we have sufficient miners to increase deep mining and the second negative then presented the PMA that we lack sufficient trained personnel, the contradiction would be obvious. (This example, incidentally, is not all that far-fetched; negatives frequently fall into inconsistencies fully this blatant.) If the first negative has not evidenced the position, many judges will allow the negative to escape by dropping one of the arguments; if the evidence is contradictory, however, most critics would consider both arguments lost.

• First Negative Options

As previously mentioned, each of the negative speeches has certain duties to perform. The first negative constructive, of course, launches the assault on the affirmative case. Only a few years ago a first negative might reasonably hope to win the debate on his own by presenting such a devastating attack on harm or inherency that the affirmative could never recover. Except with a very poor affirmative, this rarely happens today; indeed, with the increasing importance of the plan to the debate, the role of the first negative has declined while that of the second has risen dramatically in importance. Second affirmative constructives are now so well prepared that they are capable in many instances of destroying the first negative position. Thus the case side is essentially won for the affirmative, and the first negative rebuttal often becomes an exercise in futility. This decline in the ability of the first negative arguments to make a substantial impact on the debate probably played a major role in the decision of negative teams to largely abandon case attacks and emphasize the alternatives to the affirmative plan, which is the crux of modern collegiate debate (see Chapter Thirteen). This need not be so if the initial negative speaker would only take advantage of the available options.

The first negative constructive should be, in essence, a holding and probing action, intended largely to set up more powerful attacks in the first negative rebuttal. The first negative who fires his best salvos in the initial speech is doomed to the fate described above. You should question, challenge, and present evidenced attacks (but usually not with the strongest evidence) and look for weaknesses. This speech, however, should be of sufficient strength to force the second affirmative to respond with his best arguments. (He will often do so anyway regardless of the first negative's power, since by the time the debate enters rebuttals the affirmative will have no time to initiate evidenced positions.) With the full extent of the affirmative position now evident, the first negative rebuttalist can pick and choose issues. Since there are only four or five minutes to reply to the opponents' eight or ten, you probably cannot respond to everything anyway; careful analysis of the affirmative arguments allows you to drop those positions you cannot win and to charge home against those you can destroy. In essence this technique gives you as many options as possible, as late in the debate as possible. An affirmative is hurt more going into the first affirmative rebuttal by having one or two arguments destroyed than by having half a dozen merely dented. Dents may be pounded quickly back into shape. To rebuild an argument from the ground up takes time, and time is the one commodity the affirmative lacks in rebuttals.

One crucial warning should be issued. You must make certain to have introduced the arguments in constructives; since, unlike affirmative sandbagging, this procedure crosses the constructive rebuttal line. In this way you cannot legitimately be accused of presenting brand new positions in rebuttals.

For many years, especially on the college level, the counterplan was practically a dead item. With the advent of new affirmative case forms and strategies, however, the counterplan has returned to respectability. While it is often presented in a classical manner, several new mutations of it have developed; four of these seem especially prevalent.

The first is the **conditional counterplan**. This position is presented in addition to other attacks on the affirmative case and may well be in conflict with them. If, for example, a negative attacks the need and then offers a counterplan to meet the need they have been denying, they might justly be charged with inconsistency. Because the counterplan has been offered conditionally, however, the contradiction is avoided. In other words, the negative is saying to the judge, "If you don't buy our need attack, here is an entirely separate argument against the affirmative."

Many judges accept this type of argument; others do not. Those favoring the option allow it because of its conditional nature; the negative is requesting the acceptance of only one position at a time. Those opposed often reject it precisely because of that same conditional nature, arguing that an issue either is or it is not, but that it cannot be something halfway between, *i.e.*, conditional. Some game theorists maintain that this approach places too much of a burden on the affirmative. Those who wish to employ the conditional argument should know their judges, lest they merely waste time presenting a position which will be ignored from the outset.

The second unique form of the counterplan is the adoption of exactly what the affirmative has proposed, but at the state level. The negative will advocate that the fifty states and the District of Columbia, each acting separately but all acting, can achieve the same benefit the affirmative has proposed. The added advantages to this method may include such philosophical positions as better federalism or increased democracy since the level of government used is closer to the citizen. More tangible advantages which have been used are more efficient financing methods or less bureaucratic waste.

Another recent addition to the world of the counterplan is the **exclusionary counterplan**. When advancing this position, the negative advocates adopting the affirmative plan, but implementing it in fewer areas or jurisdictions than the affirmative. Since most affirmatives are required by the proposition to make a change for the entire United States, negatives may exclude one or more states, the District of Columbia, or certain specific areas throughout the country. This, of course, makes the counterplan non-topical and, therefore, legitimate. When selecting your exclusions, you should exercise caution and reasonableness; do not select exclusions which make no sense. A college negative recently put the affirmative plan into effect, "except for South Dakota."

When challenged, they could produce no logical reason for this particular exclusion. Some popular and seemingly reasonable exclusions are Alaska and Hawaii (these non-continental states often have different needs than the contiguous 48) and Indian reservations (cultural differences often make the exclusion of Native Americans from the plan's provisions quite reasonable).

Finally, negatives have developed the **delayed enactment** or studies counterplan. They will admit the harm exists but will contend that the particular solution proposed has not yet been explored or tested to a sufficient degree to warrant its adoption at this time. As an alternative, the negative will suggest that the implementation of the plan be held in abeyance for a period of time to permit a detailed and comprehensive study; usually the counterplan will mandate such an examination. Then at the end of two or three years, if the proposal is found to be of sufficient merit, it can be adopted with a much greater certainty that it will succeed. The additional advantage claimed for such a counterplan, of course, is the greater level of probability that the plan will work, based on the additional, intensive study.

The greatest danger in the use of this approach is the insistence of some judges that it is not a counter-proposition at all, but is actually the resolution. They argue that simply putting the adoption of the plan off for further study does not make it any less topical; and if the negative approves the adoption of such a plan, they are advocating the resolution and should lose. Proponents of the approach argue that the tactic is not topical because it lacks a guarantee; if the study shows the particular plan to be undesirable, the negative would not implement it; but the affirmative is committed to their plan no matter what its defects. As with many of the devices we have discussed, this one should be used only by the advanced debater who is capable of understanding its full implications.[1]

• Second Negative Options

Only a few years ago the second negative plan attacks were considered fillers to which the affirmative had to respond, thus wasting their time while the killing first negative arguments were slighted. Now, as previously mentioned, the opposite appears true; many judges view the plan attacks as the crucial points in the negative stand. Since this is the case, plan objections should be constructed with care, and the ultimate implications and extensions of initial positions fully considered.

The majority of judges view disadvantages as the most important type of plan objection. Indeed, many judges have come to demand a disadvantage in order to vote against the affirmative case. This seems to be an unnecessarily narrow requirement, since the defeat of the affirmative on any case issue or on an absolute plan-meet-advantage should be grounds for a negative ballot as well. Yet, since many do insist on a disadvantage, the wise negative will construct not only specific disadvantages to present against the specific cases which are being used, but also general disadvantages which may be used against almost any case. Examples of these are attacks on funding mechanisms which the affirmative might use to finance their plan or general philosophical objections to the nature of the proposition itself. Some of these may be only of nuisance value, but they may provide a position on which to fall back should the affirmative present a case on which you have little or no evidence.

Most judges tend to weigh or balance advantages against disadvantages and to vote for that side which has something left after all else has been balanced out. In such a situation it is wise to claim for your disadvantages, as does the wise affirmative for advantages, all the significance you can muster.

Just as the first negative may withhold the strongest evidence or extensions until the rebuttal, so also may a second negative wish to sandbag an element of a plan objection until the rebuttal, thus confounding the affirmative in their attempt to destroy the argument in first affirmative rebuttal. If, for example, the second negative withholds the strongest quantification card on a disadvantage until the rebuttal, this will almost invariably result in the first affirmative rebuttalist, who is always pressed for time, trying to dismiss the objection by claiming, "the significance was unquantified." When strong quantification appears in the last negative rebuttal, the second affirmative rebuttal is left with the unenviable task of formulating an entirely new answer to the argument in the last minutes of the debate. The warning concerning the constructive rebuttal line is even more important here; you must be certain that the argument itself is made in the second constructive even if evidence is withheld.

The order of arguments in the second negative rebuttal is often of prime importance. Since they are his arguments, the second negative will almost invariably want to spend more time on the plan objections. For this reason, and because it is usually stronger to end on one's own ground, it is probably best to begin the rebuttal with the case arguments; this assures that they will be covered. Having consulted with his partner, the second negative knows which case arguments have victory potential and thus understands what must be extended. When returning to the plan objections, it is usually best to begin with the disadvantages (remember the affinity most judges have for them) and to make certain all of them are extended in a winning manner. If there is any time left when that is done, other arguments may be handled. The only exception to this advice is when the speaker knows that the judge likes plan-meet-advantages or circumvention arguments and has a killing one sitting there waiting to be used. In all other circumstances, the rule should be disadvantages first.

An interesting strategic approach which has emerged during the last few years is the concept of **counter warrants**. This development is based on the old theory that the affirmative is not merely advocating the adoption of their specific case, but of the entire resolution. The counter warrant, therefore, argues against the adoption of the proposition *per se*, regardless of what specific plan the affirmative advances. Such an approach may be united with explicit attacks on the affirmative case or may be used by itself. This latter approach may be especially helpful if the affirmative is advancing a case which the negative is unprepared to contest.[2]

As a concluding comment, remember that the essence of the negative strategy is the attack. While not all the assaults should be at full force, you should keep pushing ahead nonetheless. The negative who sits and waits for the affirmative to make a mistake instead of going out and creating such an error in their opponent's position is in for a long and frustrating debate indeed.

NOTES

1. For a critique of the studies counterplan, see Thomas J. Hynes, Jr., "Study: Hope or False Promise," *Journal of the American Forensic Association,* XVII, 3 (Winter, 1980), pp. 192-198.

2. For contrasting views of the counter warrant approach, see James L. Paulsen and Jack L. Rhodes, "The Counter-Warrant as a Negative Strategy: A Modest Proposal," *Journal of the American Forensic Association,* XV, 4 (Spring, 1979), pp. 205-210; and Marjorie Keeshan and Walter Ulrich, "A Critique of the Counter-Warrant as a Negative Strategy," *Journal of the American Forensic Association,* XVII, 3 (Winter, 1980), pp. 199-203.

9
CHAPTER

Delivery

Many debaters and coaches would like to ignore the fact that academic debate is an exercise in speech communication. While it is true that issues and arguments are important in debating, so is the manner in which they are presented.

A debater works in a difficult communication situation. Because of the nature of propositions usually debated, the supporting material required is frequently technical and complex. It is necessary for the arguments to be presented in clearly organized logical sequences. Frequently the speaker has a great deal to say and a very limited time in which to say it. Consequently, careful attention should be given to clarity of presentation: (1) the organization of arguments, (2) the wording of arguments, and (3) the delivery of arguments.

Organization

Every debate coach has had the experience of reading over a ballot for a losing decision on which the judge comments that certain items were ignored and having the losing debater say, "I did cover those items." The debater may be correct, but obviously the arguments were presented in such a way that the judge did not know they were being covered. One way to improve the chances of a judge following what is being said is for the debater to pay close attention to how the presentation of an argument is organized. The organization of an argument, whether it be a main point in the constructive case or a rebuttal, is based on the theory that an argument is a line of reasoning or an inference from premises that is offered to support a conclusion the debater wants accepted.

A debater's main points are the primary arguments in support of the proposition and are conclusions stated as generalizations. These main arguments (points) usually should be supported by secondary arguments and generalizations which serve as explanations of the main point. These secondary arguments generally need to be supported by evidence (facts, opinions, and material objects). Arguments that are not understood will not win decisions. Clear organization of each point presented is a big step toward understanding.

The story is told of an elderly bishop who was asked by a newly ordained preacher how the old man had gained his reputation as such an excellent public speaker. The bishop replied, "It's simple. First I tell them what I am going to tell them. Then I tell them. Then I tell them what I told them." That is excellent advice for debaters, whether organizing an entire speech or just the points in a speech. Dr. Robert Huber, for many years a highly successful debate coach at the University of Vermont, gave his debaters a little jingle which echoes this advice to help them organize their points; a jingle coaches who learned their debate from Huber have continued using for the same purpose. It goes:

Name it
Explain it
Prove it
Conclude it

Name it is the wording for the main point. It is a simple, concisely worded sentence. In an outline, it would be designated by a Roman numeral.

Explain it is a clarification sentence that would be designated in the outline by capital letters.

Prove it is the specific evidence in the form of facts and opinions. In an outline the proof would be designated by Arabic numerals and small letters.

Conclude it does just that; it clearly concludes the point. This frequently is done with a sentence restating the main point.

This formula is an excellent way to organize a debate argument. Take for example this argument used in a classroom debate proposing the United States impose trade sanctions against Japan:

(name)   I. The United States will benefit from the proposed trade sanctions against Japan.

(explain)   A. It will increase pressure on Japan to stop dumping computer chips in this country.

(prove)   1. Lee Smith, *Fortune*, April 27, 1987, p. 175.

         2. William Chaze, *U. S. News and World Report*, April 27, 1987, p. 16.

(explain)   B. It will increase pressure on Japan to open her markets to U.S. exports.

(prove)   1. Stephen Krepp, *Time*, April 6, 1987, p. 50.

         2. George Russell, *Time*, April 13, 1987, p. 28.

(conclude)   C. Curtailing dumping and opening markets can only benefit the United States.

This **"NEPC" organization** of a main point can be made even more effective by the use of clear sequential patterns such as causal, chronological, topical, and criteria-satisfaction. **Causal sequences** are used to account for the existence of some phenomena with the point set up to move from present cause to future effects or the reverse, from present effects to past causes. The "NEPC" example on proposed trade sanctions against Japan is an example of the causal sequence.

The **chronological sequence** traces the development of an institution of practice during a period of time, either forward or backward. In a debate on whether censorship is a problem in the United States, one speaker used time sequence to develop the argument that censorship is a growing problem:

(name)   I. Censorship of library materials is alive and growing.

(explain)   A. According to the American Library Association, censorship throughout the United States tripled from 1979 to 1982.

(explain)   B. According to the Indiana Library Trustees Association, censorship attempts increased in Indiana between 1984 and 1986.

(prove)   1. In 1984, there were 33 formal challenges against library materials.

            2. In 1985, the challenges had increased to 41.

            3. In 1986, there were 58

formal challenges.

(explain) C. According to the Washington-based People for the American Way, not only had there been a 20% rise in censorship causes during the 1986-87 school year, but a rise in successful attempts.

(prove)   1. Out of the 50 attempts of censorship in the 13-state Midwest area, 25 cases, two from Indiana, had been successful.

2. Of the 153 attempts at censorship in 41 states, 103 had been successful.

(conclude) D. Censorship is on the rise here in Indiana and throughout the United States.

Many subject areas can be broken down to a subject-matter pattern or what is called a topical sequence. **Topical sequence** is based on standard categories or natural divisions of a subject and is an excellent sequence to use in developing either a series of arguments or a single argument. For instance, the federal government might be arranged in executive, legislative, and judicial branches; taxes as local, state, and federal or as income, sales, and property; minority groups might well be arranged as Chicano, Black, and Indian. An example of using topical sequence to organize a single argument is the following one from the previously mentioned censorship debate:

(name)	I. According to *CAUTION! Books Challenged or Banned in 1983–1984,* many organizations are trying to get certain books censored or banned in our public schools.
(explain)	A. They are trying to get certain elementary books censored.
(prove)	1. *The Wizard of Oz* by Frank Baum.
	a. It portrays a witch as good.
	b. It portrays certain traits as personaity developed rather than God- given.
	2. *Cinderella.*
	3. *Mother Goose Nursery Rhymes.*
	4. *It's Fun to Rob a Wig —* barred because it told the story of a puppy who liked to take wigs.
(explain)	B. They are trying to get certain middle school books censored.
(prove)	1. *Diary of Anne Frank.*
	2. Most of Judy Blume's books.
	a. *Are You There, God? It's Me, Margaret.*
	b. *Blubber.*
	c. *Then Again, Maybe I Won't.*
(explain)	C. They are trying to get certain

secondary books censored.

(explain)
1. *Grapes of Wrath* by John Steinbeck.
2. *Of Mice and Men* by John Steinbeck.

(prove)
3. *The Adventures of Huckleberry Finn* by Mark Twain.
4. *Lord of the Flies* by William Golding.

D. You may not agree with what is happening but many books in our public schools are being censored or are in the process

(conclude)
of being censored.

Criteria-satisfaction is an effective sequence to prove a problem exists by defining the problem. Notice how a speaker arguing the proposition, "Marion County's legal system concerning drunk drivers needs improvement," defines the problem with a criteria-satisfaction sequence:

(name)
I. What are the criteria for an effective legal system concerning drunk drivers?

(explain)
A. An effective system should include laws that truly punish the offender.

(prove)
1. Sarasota County, Florida, uses bumper stickers to punish drunk drivers. (*Time*, June 17, 1985, p. 52.)
2. Mandatory jail sentences

would punish drunk driv-
ers. (Sally Nelson, inter-
view, 12/8/86.)

(explain)   B. An effective system should
include laws that provide for
correction of the offender's
problem.

(prove)   1. The DWI prisons in Ari-
zona, Maryland, and Bos-
ton provide effective correction for the offender's
problem. (Scott Clark, in-
terview, 11/16/87.)

     2. Probation officers trained
to counsel for alcoholism
would provide effective
correction for the of-
fender's problem. (Clark,
11/16/ 87.)

(conclude)   C. There are effective systems
concerning drunk drivers.

(name)   II. How does Marion County's legal
system fail these criteria?

(explain)   A. The laws do not effectively
punish offenders.

(prove)   1. First time DWI conviction
is a slap on the wrist.
(Clark.)

     2. Sentences are often sus-
pended.

     3. DWI's with suspended li-
cense often drive anyway.

(explain)   B. The system does not provide
effective correction for the
problem.

(prove)

    1. Judges are too easy on offenders.

    2. Probation officers are not trained to counsel for alcoholism.

    3. Habitual offenders are too common.

(conclude)   C. Marion County's legal system does not meet the criteria for an effective system concerning drunk drivers.

Debaters should not only organize points carefully, but also should use definite stylistic devices to focus the judge's attention on the points being made. One such technique is to use initial summaries stated in concise, clearly worded sentences. For example, the final affirmative rebuttal speaker might take a few seconds and tell the judge, "There are four excellent reasons for rejecting the negative stand in this debate: 1....., 2....., 3....., 4..... ." This preview helps the judge focus on the forthcoming arguments.

Another clarifying technique is transitions notifying the judge that one point is finished, and the speaker is now moving to another argument. Use short phrases such as, "Let us now examine our second argument." It can be done in a few seconds and the judge is not caught trying to continue flowing a point that has been completed. Judges like to know when a speaker is through with one argument and is moving to another.

Not all arguments carry the same weight,

nor does all evidence have the same importance. It is a good habit to signpost arguments and to alert the judge to especially vital points. Use phrases such as: "The main thrust of the negative argument was ....., but did *you* notice this .....?"; "Please compare these statistics with those presented by the affirmative."; or "The most compelling reason for rejecting this argument is ..... ." In other words, the wise debater makes it as easy as possible for the judge or audience to follow the arguments. The easier you make it for the listener to follow your argument, the less likely you are to have to say, "But I did cover that point."

Wording

What we say is, and should be, the most important aspect of debating; our wording is all too frequently neglected in preparing for the debate. One of the lasting values of participating in an educational debate program could and should be the improved command of spoken language. So let us now discuss the second phase in developing clarity in presentation— wording our ideas. One of the important distinctions between the spoken and written word is the necessity for instant intelligibility in oral communication. In a debate the speaker gets one chance with the listener. Either the listener (translate judge or audience) understands what is being said immediately or not at all. There is no time to stop, look up a word in the dictionary, mull it over a bit, and then go on listening.

Parading your vocabulary may impress some people, but if a judge misses the meaning of the word he will not be impressed with your argument. Obfuscate is a good word; but it calls for a distinctiveness of articulation that dim, darken, confuse, or becloud do not. Prevaricator is not nearly as forceful a word as liar. Ursine may be a more interesting word than bearlike, but a goodly number of people do not have it in their working vocabulary.

Language that is easy to understand should be simple, descriptive, yet not draw attention away from the content itself. Simple language is achieved by using the specific, the concrete, and the short word whenever possible while avoiding compound, complex sentences.

Accurate words are those which suggest the speaker's meaning with precision. Mark Twain once remarked, "that the difference between the right word and the almost right word is like the difference between lightning and the lightning bug." As a rule, the accurate word is the specific word rather than a general word. Criminal is a general word; rapist, pickpocket, and thief are specific words.

Concrete terms are those which refer to real things— things which can be seen, felt, or heard— thus making the specific even more accurate. For instance, using Irish Setter for Setter, and Pope Paul for "the Pope."

The **short word**, like the short sentence, gives a forcefulness to language that can be persuasive. Misrepresentation is a longer and less forceful word than is false.

At the same time you are striving for simple, easy-to-understand language, you should not forget the necessity for adding **vividness** to what you are saying. An ancient Arab proverb holds "that is the best description which makes the ear an eye." We can make the ear an eye when clarity is achieved by the use of analogies, metaphors, similes, and words that have the capability of stirring the imagination of the listener while at the same time clarifying by implied comparison or contrast. Lincoln used such a stylistic device effectively when he built a speech, one of his most famous, around a metaphor from the Bible, "A house divided against itself cannot stand." During the 1984 presidential campaign an anti-abortion speaker used a one-sentence analogy effectively when he compared the stand of the Democrat vice-president nominee, Ferraro, on abortion with somebody in the days of slavery saying, "I'm personally opposed to slavery, but I don't care if the people down the street want to own slaves." It took the speaker a few seconds to present the analogy; it took Ms. Ferraro several attempts at refuting it before it dropped from the campaign. An attorney was using a simile when he argued against the closing of a branch library by saying that "putting a padlock on the library is like putting a padlock on the mind."

You should avoid one type of figurative language, however, the cliche. **Cliches** are simply figurative phrases which from overuse have lost their impact. Use jargon with discretion, although with the proper audience it is acceptable. Debaters have adopted all kinds of language shortcuts to save a few precious seconds, and the use of debate jargon is understood clearly by other debaters and most judges. The problem arises when the debaters put on a program before the local Rotary Club and keep telling the audience to "go to the top of the flow" or "now look at the second DA."

The spoken word is an essential part of debating. Failing to develop clarity of language is failing to develop one's full potential as a debater. The extent of a debater's speaking vocabulary depends entirely upon the effort spent in building it. If you become word conscious and you use your debate practice sessions to improve how you word your arguments as well as how you develop and defend them; your clarity of expression can only improve.

The story is told of how William Jennings Bryan, one of this country's greatest orators, once gave some excellent advice to a group of seminary students— advice that nicely ties up what this chapter has been trying to say about effectiveness of language. One of the young men asked Bryan if he had any advice to give would-be public speakers. Bryan simply replied, "I Corinthians, 14:9," and walked away. The young seminarians hurried to their rooms, opened their King James version of the Bible to I Corinthians 14:9, and read, "Except as ye utter by the tongue language easy to understand, how shall it be known what is spoken."

Delivery

The third phase in developing clarity of presentation is delivery. The cumulative evidence of innumerable studies is that there is a definite correlation between quality of delivery and the successful communication of information and ideas. Studies dealing with attitude change have concluded that effectiveness in the delivery contributes not only to the credibility of the speaker but also to the persuasiveness of the speaker in achieving acceptance of the message. Listening studies and countless critic judges have demonstrated that an attentive listener can comprehend and flow up to two hundred words per minute. However, rapid fire speakers should be aware that a fast rate of delivery places a premium upon clear organization, careful word choice, clear articulation, variety of emphasis, and adaption of volume to the room in which the debate is being held. Rapid delivery in itself is acceptable to a judge accustomed to such practice, but even the most experienced judge will have difficulty in following poorly worded and poorly organized arguments delivered in a monotonous, slurred manner with the volume too loud or too low for the room and at a rate that permits little time to comprehend what is being said.

Debaters should be aware that the effectiveness of their delivery is determined by how they sound and how they look while speaking. Even the most tolerant of judges cannot help but be influenced by how they hear what is being said and what they see while it is being said. Many judges correlate sloppy language and sloppy appearance with sloppy thinking. There are judges, just as there are audiences, who will even accept an inferior argument over a superior one because of the manner in which it was delivered. Rare indeed are the examples of debaters who have lost points for excellence in delivery.

Speaking well is a learned process. Every one of us has learned to speak. How well we speak depends primarily upon how well we learned to do so. Barring physical or mental defects, and these are comparatively rare, all of us can learn to speak effectively in public. Debaters should use practice debates to help develop good speech habits. Tape record or, even better, video tape practices and play them back for critical analysis of the arguments and presentation.

Some practical suggestions for improving delivery are the following:

1. Develop good breathing habits and **breath control** while speaking. The secret to a good speaking voice begins with a relaxed throat and sufficient breath properly controlled. This is an ability nearly all of us can acquire by practice if we have not already acquired it while growing up.

2. Work on **articulation**, **enunciation**, and **pronunciation**. Clarity in the English language is largely dependent upon clear con-

sonant sounds, so take special care with enunciation of final consonants. If the recorder indicates a general tendency toward careless articulation, a fun way to correct the problem is to become adept with various tongue twisters such as "Peter Piper picked a peck of pickled peppers....," etc. If you have trouble pronouncing a word, look it up in the dictionary, get the correct pronunciation, and practice it until you know it well.

3. Work at developing a **pitch** and **volume** of voice that is comfortable for you and one you can adapt to various size rooms and audiences. Be aware that as rate increases pitch has a tendency to increase. Develop the habit of projecting your voice without straining it so it can easily be heard by the people in the back row.

4. An excellent way to gain variety of emphasis and rate is to **pause** just before starting a new point and to consciously reduce the rate of speaking as you begin each main point. The few seconds you lose will more than be offset by the clarity you gain. During practice, work at varying the rate with which you present various arguments so that you will be likely to do the same thing in the heat of a close debate. Work at putting added stress on key words in a sentence.

5. Vocalized pauses and overused expressions such as O.K. for a conclusion or transition are habits which are broken only by becom-

ing aware of them. This is another excellent reason for taping practices and playing them back. Once you start hearing these bad habits, you are well on the way to eliminating them.

6. Develop good platform habits. Maintain eye contact with your audience, even if it is only one judge and, hopefully, a timekeeper.

Get in the habit of using a variety of **gestures**. Spontaneous gestures give added meaning to what you are saying. This will probably mean moving to one side of the lectern and not hunching over your flowsheet and cards.

Avoid distracting from what you are saying by playing with pieces of chalk, pens, or pencils while speaking. Also avoid nose scratching, ear pulling, and other meaningless actions.

Whether it is an audience debate or a tournament debate, debaters are speaking to get a favorable response. It may be to persuade an audience to believe a certain way; it may be to persuade a judge to vote the right way; but the debater is after a response. The evidence is strong for believing that clear, attention-holding delivery can facilitate a more deliberative appraisal of argumentative structure and proof than does poor delivery. Frequently when the better case loses, it is because it was poorly presented and thus imperfectly understood.

Debate is today as good public address has always been— not only analysis and issues; not only evidence and reasoning; not only organization, language and style; and certainly not only delivery, but all of them combined. The able debater is an able speaker debating well.[1]

NOTES

1. James H. McBath and Nicholas M. Cripe, "Delivery: Rhetoric's Rusty Canon," *Journal of the American Forensic Association*, II (January, 1965), p. 2.

10
CHAPTER

Refutation and Strategy

Refutation is the process of building up your own case and tearing down that of the opponent. In reality this is a singular process since the accomplishment of one of these tasks automatically achieves the other. The process of refutation is one of the most difficult debate skills to learn, involving as it does critical listening, rapid thinking, and fluent communication. Only diligent practice will create an accomplished rebuttalist.

Flowing

The first step in good refutation is an accurate and detailed knowledge of what the opposition has said; this, in turn, is composed of two other skills– careful listening and detailed recording. You need to develop the ability to listen carefully and critically, noting the strengths and weaknesses of opposing arguments as they are presented. It is impossible to remember, especially in a complex debate, all that has transpired; therefore, you must develop the ability to flow the round. To flow is to record in outline form what each speaker has said.

The flow is kept, logically enough, on a **flowsheet**, usually a legal pad turned sideways or a medium-sized art pad. The first affirmative speech, in outline form but with as much detail as possible, is then recorded down the left-hand margin. Opposite each of the contentions and issues is then recorded what the first negative has said against it; if nothing is said against a particular argument, the space next to it is left blank. This procedure is continued throughout the debate. Naturally, you will prepare your own column on the flowsheet before getting up to speak. It has become common for debaters to use colored pens (red and blue, for instance) to designate which column represents which side.

Several techniques may be helpful in learning to flow. You should not try to crowd everything on one sheet of paper. If it fits there, fine; if it does not, then as many sheets as necessary should be used.   Since the first negative and the second affirmative will often have more to say on specific points than the first affirmative, it is a good idea to leave plenty of space between contentions of the original affirmative case. This will prevent overcrowding and allow one to flow arguments opposite those which they are intended to refute. The plan is usually flowed separately, either on the back of the sheet containing the case or on a different sheet of paper. The plan objections and their answers and extensions may then be flowed next to the plan.

When recording what is being said, every effort should be made to get down as much detail as possible. At a very minimum the organizational pattern should be recorded, the major headings and their subordinate arguments listed, and evidence noted. As you become more skilled, more detail should appear. Instead of just indicating evidence, try to get down who said it, what they said, and the date on which it was said. All of these will be useful in refutation techniques discussed below. The use of symbols and a personal version of shorthand will speed up the process. Usually only you and your partner will need to read the flow; as long as you can do so, it matters little if the sheet is illegible to others. A few examples of such symbols are:

= and its opposite =

> for greater than, or

< for less than

↑ for increasing, or

↓ for decreasing.

Some symbols and abbreviations will come from the logic of the topic itself as certain issues, ideas, or words become common during the year. The more you get down accurately, the better job you can do in refutation.

Refutation Techniques

The process of refutation itself almost always involves one or more of these three activities: countering the opposition's evidence, destroying the link between the evidence and the argument, and tearing apart the reasoning used.

Dealing with the opposition's evidence may take either of two forms: discovering something faulty with the evidence itself or countering it with other evidence. Both, of course, may be employed on one argument. First, the **opposing evidence should be tested** to discover if it has any serious flaws; refer here to the tests for evidence discussed in Chapter Five. If the opposition's proof is deficient, it may be exposed for what it is and any impact it may have had quickly dies. In such a case it may not be necessary to bring up any evidence against that presented. In many instances, however, the other team's evidence will not have any particular problems; it will conform to generally accepted standards for proof. In such a case it must be countered with opposing evidence; there are four ways in which this may be done.

First, you may **match the opposition** citation for citation, presenting a piece of evidence for each piece they bring up. This is a legitimate method of refutation when the opposition needs merely to be neutralized since they have the greater burden of proof; thus, it may be employed by the negative in responding to a requirement of an affirmative case, such as significance or by the affirmative when replying to a plan objection. In either of these cases neutralization, which equals a tie, is sufficient to win the point. It is an inadequate response in those instances when you must establish superiority of position, such as inherency on the affirmative case.

Secondly, you may **overwhelm the opposition** with the amount of your evidence, presenting several citations to each one of theirs. This is recommended as a reasonable method if you have the greater burden on the particular issue or if the opponent's one source is particularly strong. Here you are saying, in essence, that although the opposition has one person who contends yes, our team has half a dozen who say no; the preponderance of evidence is on our side.

Thirdly, you may present a **superior source**. The affirmative cites a Congressman who gives his opinion in favor of their position; you, in return, cite an expert who has thirty years experience in the field and who is the author of ten books on the subject. Clearly, you have the more competent authority; and when the evidence on the point is weighed, the balance should come down on your side.   In making use of this method, you should be sure to point out explicitly the superiority of your authority.

Finally, you may counter evidence by bringing up a **more recent source**, or updating.   This technique is frequently used in debates and not always legitimately, for greater recency does not always mean a better source; it all depends on the issue being contested. If an historical fact is in doubt, for example the date of a certain event of the last century, it usually makes little difference whether an historian from 1900 is cited or one from 1975; the facts probably will not have changed. On the other hand, if the issue being contested concerns the current status of a Supreme Court ruling, recency may be all important.   Therefore, you must make sure when using this technique or when it is used by the opposition, that recency is a legitimate response.   As with superior source, you should indicate when presenting the material how recency places the greater strength with your side of the argument.

The second major means of refutation

after examination of evidence is exploration of the **link between the opposition's evidence and their argument**. Here one simple question is the basis of analysis: Does the evidence say what the opposition claims it says? In many instances teams will claim a strong position on an issue basic to their case, read a piece of evidence, and then conclude that they have substantiated their point. Careful examination of the evidence, however, reveals that it comes nowhere close to proving what has been claimed in the argument. You should listen carefully to the evidence, especially when what is claimed seems too good to be true; it often is. A debater not certain what the evidence said should ask to see the card. You should not let an opponent get away with basing analysis on evidence which does not really support the position taken.

Finally, refutation may be directed at the opposition's **reasoning**. All too often, even if the evidence is valid and it is linked to the argument, the reasoning process itself is faulty. A claimed causal link may be only correlational; an analogy may lack similarity in the vital aspects; a generalization may be based on an inadequate sample; and so forth. Essential to successful analysis of the opposition's reasoning is familiarity with the tests for the important forms of reasoning.

Organizing Refutation

In conducting refutation you need to be certain the judge understands four items: Where you are in the organizational pattern; what the specific argument being refuted is; what the exact nature of the refutation is; and how this response defeats the original position. A debater who omits any of these steps risks losing the effect of the refutation.

Usually your position on the flow will be clear, since most debaters go straight down the arguments. Nevertheless, it is usually a good idea to indicate by number and letter where you are, such as "II B 2." Secondly, a brief label should be given to the argument being contested; if possible, this should be the same as that originally presented by whomever introduced the point into the debate, since this is more than likely what the judge has written down. An example might be "states lack the authority." Thirdly, the point being made should be announced and then evidenced. Many debaters make the mistake of announcing what argument is being refuted and then immediately launching into their evidence. This misses the crucial step of indicating exactly what point they are offering in refutation. You should present the heading first and then read the card, as "no, the states do have statutory authority, as the *Harvard Law Review* indicates, etc." This gives the judge something to write down on the flow and then supports the position.

Finally, in a step most debaters neglect, the argument should be clinched by showing how this position defeats the opponent. For example, "we have an evidenced update of the affirmative position" indicates exactly what has been done. Only when you have mastered this four step process can you be reasonably sure that your refutation is effective.

The advancing of one's own position, after it has been presented and then attacked is called **extending the argument**. An extension is the moving forward of an original argument in such a way that it takes into account or neutralizes the opposition's response. An extension is not a shift in position; such a shift is almost universally held to be an illegitimate debate tactic. Rather, it clarifies the full implications of the original stance and explains with logic and evidence how the opposition's intervening remarks fail to undermine the truth of this position. Learning to extend effectively is another of the difficult facets of debate and is best discovered by listening to those who are skilled in its use and then by practicing until you gain the ability for yourself.

Refutation Strategies

As with many competitive activities, debate often becomes a contest of strategies in which outwitting opponents becomes as important as outplaying them. Knowledge of some of the basic strategies is important to debaters not only in the offensive sense (using them), but from a defensive posture (protecting against them) as well. There is not space here to present all the strategies possible in a debate, but a few of the major ones will be discussed.

There are two important points to remember when considering the use of these or any other strategies. First, they should not be used just for the sake of using them; there must be a definite purpose in their employment. Debaters who use a technique simply because it sounds clever, rather than because it fits their particular skills, may be working with their own weaknesses and opening themselves to their opponent's strengths. Secondly, many judges are suspicious of devices which smack of strategy or cleverness, even going so far as to vote against them out of prejudice. Prudent debaters become aware of judges' biases and are careful when employing such strategies in front of them.

The first, the most elementary, and the most important strategy is actually a form of audience analysis. In keeping with the above paragraph, it is the basis of all decisions, strategic or otherwise. It is this: KNOW YOUR JUDGE. Knowing who the **judge** is, what case his team employs, what he likes or will permit, and what he will not allow may save numerous difficulties and assist you in achieving more than might be done by simple skill in the round. A debate does not take place in the verbalizing of the speakers; it certainly does not take place on their flowsheets; and it does not even take place on the judge's flow. If there is a cardinal precept which should be indelibly engraved in the mind of every debater, it is that *the debate takes place in the mind of the judge*. It does not matter what you think happened in the round, and to some extent it does not matter what the judge has written down. What he or she perceives to have happened, did— at least as far as victory or defeat is concerned.

Just as an effective public speaker analyzes the audience and then adapts the speech to the analysis, so does the wise debater analyze the judge and make use of that analysis. If you know, for example, that a particular judge does not understand the most basic of economic concepts, it would be silly to employ economic arguments in front of that critic; if you are aware that a judge detests the spread, you should slow down; and if it becomes clear during a speech that the judge is thoroughly lost, you should make an effort to clarify. You must adapt, be observant, use feedback, and, insofar as possible, make sure the judge understands your position on the crucial issues in the debate. By knowing the judge and being aware of his likes and dislikes, you can from time to time add a debate to the victory column which otherwise might not have been there; and that, after all, is what the competitive aspect of this activity is all about.

Some squads go so far as to keep a judge file, a series of cards on which are listed the proclivities and quirks of various judges frequently encountered. Before a round in which a particular individual is scheduled to judge, the team can refresh their memories about which techniques are liable to be most successful. The best method of obtaining the necessary information about judges is from previous ballots. All too many teams simply skim over their decisions, accepting any praise and laughing off critical comments before consigning the ballots to the trash. A more fruitful activity is to analyze carefully the reasons for decision and glean from them what a given judge wants. You may disagree violently with what a particular judge expects, but if you hope to win a decision, it is best to present the material that judge desires. The wise debate team, like the good public speaker, adapts to the audience.

This knowledge of judges may be most helpful when an opportunity arises to accept or reject certain critics, such as in an elimination round. If little is known or remembered about the individuals in question, no rational decision can be made on whether to retain them or not.

Just as the judge should be known, so also should the opposing team. During the course of a season, you are likely to encounter the same team several times. By learning early in the season what their strengths and weaknesses are and what type of case or attacks they are likely to use, you will be better prepared to meet them. Some individuals hold that attempting to find out what type of case another team is running is a highly questionable tactic. Many, however, see nothing immoral in this practice, considering it, as do athletic teams and coaches, good strategy.

Debate is very much a team activity.

Although this fact may seem obvious, it often appears that some of the participants forget it during the heat of a round. Not only do colleagues contradict, but they seem not to have listened to each other's speeches and often fail to extend crucial arguments originated by their partner. The best way to avoid such disasters is to confer strategically during the debate. This does not mean talking constantly to your partner; some teams do this to such an extent that they miss what the opponents are saying. Rather, it is careful consultation at crucial points in the round. The most helpful times are before each of the last three rebuttals. The old saying that two heads are better than one is often valid before the first affirmative rebuttal, as both debaters contribute to what will appear in that vital presentation. The second affirmative is especially helpful here, since that person is probably more familiar with the case extensions. Perhaps the most important conference is held before the 2NR when the second negative is briefed by his partner concerning the crucial arguments on the case side of the flow. The last talismans will also benefit from consultation on the meaning of some of the plan objection answers.

In each of these situations the preparation is best handled as follows: the debater about to speak concentrates first on his own area of expertise; then when finished, he so indicates to his partner, who briefs him on the other areas of importance. It is vital that both individuals not try to think, talk, and write at the same time. A rapid, but organized procedure is essential, given the limited time usually available at that point in the debate.

As mentioned in previous chapters, it is a good idea to think in advance concerning the possible arguments which an opponent might raise and then to prepare responses to those arguments. Such prepared arguments are called **blocks** or briefs; they are arguments written out, complete with evidence, transitions, and headings, so that the speaker may be precise in his wording and may save valuable time. The use of such blocks is a most helpful device.

A couple of warnings should be issued about their use, however. Some judges do not care at all for blocks, believing that "plastic sheets" indicate a lack of thought in the round and an inflexibility which destroys the quick thinking that debate should produce. You should learn which judges in your area hold such views and be sparing in the use of blocks in their rounds.

Secondly, the fears of such judges are sometimes accurate. Debaters often get so involved in reading multiple responses to opposing arguments that they miss the crux of what has been said. Consequently, speakers should not make the mistake of depending so much on their prepared arguments that they fail to think about what the opposition is doing. Blocks are an aid to refutation, not a substitute for clear thinking in the round.

Finally, comments should be made about the **spread**, which has become almost a universal in modern debate. Unfortunately, not all debaters who use the device are good at it; they use it only because they think it is chic or because they are told that they must spread in order to win. Both approaches are wrong. Like any other device, it should be used strategically to gain the best effect from it. In addition to being overused, spreading is also misunderstood. Most debaters believe that it is talking as fast as one can. While it is true that a good spread often necessitates rapid speech, the two are not at all the same thing. A spread is the presentation of multiple independent arguments in response to the opposition's points. For example, if the affirmative presents an inherency position, the negative may respond with four separate reasons why the inherency is not true. Each of these is a reason to reject the inherency, and all four must be defeated in order for the affirmative to carry their position. The affirmative might then respond multiply to each of the negative's arguments, presenting three responses to the first, two to the second, etc., by way of a counterspread. Thus, by the last two rebuttals, the entire debate may hinge on one seemingly minor point, say the second affirmative response to the negative's third response to the original inherency position. Such a complex situation has vast potential for disaster and confusion; to prevent both, several techniques are desirable.

First, clear organization is imperative; the smart speaker signposts an argument thus making sure the judge knows what is going on. Secondly, clear articulation is necessary; the best speakers are not those who speak the most rapidly, but those who can be most clearly understood at high speed. It does little good to mushmouth your way through an argument in which only one word in ten is comprehended. Thirdly, variety should be employed in order to emphasize crucial issues. Changes in rate (yes, actually slowing down for a moment), pitch, and volume can be used to tell the judge that something vital is about to be said. Lastly, the judge should be told when an argument is important. However, you should learn not to overuse this technique or, as with the boy who cried "wolf," it will lose its impact. Some debaters call every minor subpoint "crucial" so that when they reach a truly important argument they have nothing left to say.

Finally, you should remember that the spread is only one way to approach a debate. It does not have to be employed in order to win nor does its use automatically guarantee success. If it fits your skills, utilize it. If you lack some needed ability, it is probably better not to attempt the technique than to use it in mediocre fashion.

Again, the effective use of refutation and strategy is among the most difficult of debate skills to master, involving as it does critical listening; rapid thinking; solid understanding of the rules of evidence and reasoning; correct knowledge of judges and opponents; and fluent communication. Only diligent practice will create an accomplished rebuttalist.

11
CHAPTER

Cross-Examination

Cross-examination[1] was a feature of high school debate long before it was included at the college level. This aspect of the activity has great potential, but it all too often degenerates into quibbling, unpleasantness, and meaninglessness. Because of the frequently sorry state of cross-examination, a number of college coaches opposed its introduction at their level. Yet the problem is not really with the exercise itself, but with the misuse of it by those who do not understand it. Properly used cross-examination can be helpful to all those engaged in the argumentative process.

What Cross-Exam Is Not

Given the above indictment, it is first necessary to stress what cross-examination is not. It is not a chance to emulate an outstanding fictional attorney, exposing opponents' weaknesses with one brilliant stroke and winning the debate single-handedly. Any team poor enough to permit such an action could have been easily defeated otherwise, and the debater who tries to elicit the one damaging admission usually ends up wasting time. Further, cross-examination is not an opportunity to prove, at one and the same time, one's own cleverness and the opponents' stupidity. The student who goes into the cross-examination period trying to make opponents appear ignorant usually manages only to make himself appear obnoxious.

Cross-examination is not, in spite of much practical evidence to the contrary, an exercise in the avoidance of answering questions. It is only the inexperienced or mediocre debater who boasts that the opposition will secure no information. The talented or skillful speaker realizes that careful, direct answers can often do more good than harm. Finally, it must be realized that cross-examination is not an end in itself. Arguments *per se* should not be made during the period; many judges are displeased if they are. Rather, it is a time to elicit information and to clarify, thus setting up the points which are to be made in later speeches.

What Cross-Exam Is

If the above are not the purposes of cross-examination, what function does this activity serve? First, it may **clarify or gain information**. Often there will be material in opposition speeches which is not clear. Perhaps they have a plank in their plan which defies rational interpretation; perhaps they have badly misconstrued an argument; or perhaps they have used unfamiliar terminology. Whatever is causing the confusion may well be cleared up in the question periods.

Additionally, the periods may be used to **focus the debate**. There are, obviously, many more potential issues in any debate than may actually be contested. By discovering exactly which of these issues the opposition is going to press, the debater can avoid wasting time and confusing the debate by overcluttering it. In a similar vein, cross-examination may be used to **avoid traps** or sandbags. For example, if the affirmative has read off a long list of potential harms in the first constructive speech, it is legitimate for the negative cross-examiner to attempt to pin the respondent down as to which of these harms will be defended later in the debate. Most judges view this as a legitimate query and expect a reasonable, truthful answer.

Most importantly, the cross-examination period should be used to **set up later refutation**. As was discussed in Chapter Ten, the three major areas for refutation are evidence, link of evidence to argument, and reasoning. Each of these may be explored in cross-examination, and the material thereby gained may prove most helpful in the following speech. If a source seems unqualified, if the evidence does not actually say what the opposition claims it does, or if a vital link is missing from a logical construction, questioning can point it out; and the period will have served a valuable function.

Duties of the Questioner

Both the questioner and the respondent have opportunities and responsibilities during the cross-examination. We will first examine the role of the questioner.

No wise debater would get up to speak without having a good idea of what to say; why, then, do so many debaters arise to cross-examine their opponents having given not a thought concerning what they want to ask? The cross-examination should be planned out ahead of time just as are refutation blocks. More lines of questions should be prepared than can be covered in three minutes; then if one line proves useless or gets used up more quickly than expected, the debater will still have material to employ. As previously indicated, major admissions should not be expected; if the opponents admit they do not have inherency or that disadvantages lack significance, they probably could have been beaten anyway. Rather, one should probe for weaknesses, explore uncertainties, and indicate deficiencies; more will be accomplished in this manner than by striving for the one killing answer. In the same vein, the debater ought to ask questions in series, rather than trying to put everything into one **query**. A series of sharp, specific requests will be far harder to evade, will tend to elicit more, and will look far better to the judge than one giant question on which the opponent can talk forever. The inexperienced questioner may ask, "Isn't your quotation from Jones invalid?" The experienced debater would elicit more by a chain of questions such as: "Whom did you cite on contention IIA?" "Who is Jones?" "What are his credentials?" "How did he arrive at that conclusion?" "What method did he employ?" At the end of this chain the point is much more clearly made.

The cross-examination period is the questioner's offensive time; he has both the right and responsibility to retain control of the period. If the opponent tries to gain control by asking questions or by unnecessarily prolonging an answer, the questioner should remind everyone, politely, that he is the one asking the questions. This will seem even more legitimate if the above advice on clear specific questions is followed. Finally, the questioner must learn through experience when to press and when to drop a line of questioning. Sometimes it becomes clear that the respondent is simply not going to say what one wants him to, even when it is obvious to all what ought to be said. The debater should stop wasting time and get on to something else. The opponent's obstreperousness will be clear to the judge, and the point at issue can be made in the next speech. On the other hand, debaters sometimes press right to the brink of a damaging admission and then drop the material for something else. If the respondent appears willing to answer, the questioner should by all means continue.

An attorney once compared cross-examination to shaving corned beef: Don't try to cut too much off with each question. Slowly move your opponent along a continuum and never ask a final "Perry Mason" question, "So you agree?" Use the answers and come to the desired conclusion in your next speech. If you ask, the questioner will only deny the conclusion.

Duties of the Respondent

The respondent also has duties to fulfill. It is his or her responsibility to answer the questions as reasonably and directly as possible. Not only does equivocation look bad; but if one is confident in one's position, there is no reason not to respond clearly. The debaters who make a "he'll never get anything out of me" game of the cross-examination period are doing more damage to themselves and to the activity than they are to their opponents. This advice on answering holds true even for damaging admissions.

The debater may be pushed on a weak argument in the case so that it reaches the point where the deficiency is there for all to see. If it becomes clear that one cannot avoid the obvious without being ridiculous, it is probably better to make the admission openly. The more casual one is about it, the less important it will seem to be, and the damage may well be reparable in the next speech. The more one "hems and haws," the clearer it will become that one is desperately trying to hide something.

Sometimes it is necessary to qualify an answer. For example, an affirmative has indicated that they will impose restrictions if certain events happen. The negative questioner, attempting to clarify, asks, "Will you impose wage and price controls?" Neither a blunt "yes" nor an absolute "no" is correct in this situation; the respondent should answer, "Under the conditions specified in the plan, yes." The **qualifier** should always be inserted before the answer proper, lest a sharp questioner cut the respondent off before the answer is finished.

In spite of the fact that the period is supposed to be the questioner's time, there is nothing wrong in the respondent trying to take control of the situation if the questioner is foolish enough to let it happen. If an opportunity arises naturally for the respondent to ask a question in response to an opponent's query, you probably should do so. If the opponent responds, the point should be explored. This usually will enhance the respondent's **ethos** and will create a psychological superiority which will be valuable throughout the round.

Use of Cross-Exam

For both participants, use should be made of the cross-examination after it has been completed. If a respondent has promised to look up a piece of evidence and either read it or give it to the opposition, he should make certain to do so. Promises made in cross-examination should be kept. If the questioner has gained valuable admissions or raised damaging material in the period, he or his colleague should be certain to use it later during their speeches. Many judges will count material elicited in cross-examination only if something is then made of it afterwards.

Cross-examination may serve an especially valuable function for the affirmative after the second negative constructive. By clearing away a lot of the deadwood in the plan objections, much time may be saved the poor pressed first affirmative rebuttalist. Negatives will often throw in time wasters— observations or brief arguments at the start of their speech which they know they cannot win, but which they hope will occupy enough of the first affirmative rebuttalist's time so that he cannot get to more damaging disadvantages or back to the case. An affirmative question such as "What evidence was presented under the first plan objection?" is quite effective if no proof was offered. In addition, valuable linkages may be established by short queries such as: "Doesn't plan objection three rest on the assumption of double digit inflation?" "Doesn't the second disadvantage rest on the assumption of double digit inflation?" or "PMA three and disadvantage two say the same thing, don't they?" If the affirmative team uses such questioning prior to the rebuttal period, the first affirmative rebuttalist is frequently able to dispose of two opposition arguments with one response. By carefully using the cross-examination period, the affirmative can clear away a lot of material and may even set up short, but winning, answers to some of the major plan objections.

Finally, a note must be added about interpersonal relations in the cross-examination. Judges, for the most part, do not like impolite behavior, and some go so far as to mark off rather severely for it. Therefore, in the interest not only of one's general reputation, but of competitive success as well, debaters must remain polite, especially in the cross-examination period. It is sometimes difficult to be nice, especially if your opponent is violating all the rules of good behavior. But if you hold your temper, do not lower yourself to the opponent's level, and allow yourself to benefit from the contrast in personalities; you will probably enhance your ethos with all members of the debate community.

NOTES

1. For the definitive article on cross examination see Bill Henderson, "A System of Teaching Cross Examination Techniques," *Communication Education*, XXVII, 2 (March, 1978), pp. 112-118.

12
CHAPTER

Judging

The judge is one of the most crucial elements in debate; without him or her there would be no contest. In spite of this importance, however, no aspect of debate is so often criticized. Judges suffer labels, sometimes with justification, such as inconsistent, biased, ignorant of procedures, and inattentive. The person who wishes to be a good judge must carefully study the theory of argumentation and then consistently and impartially apply these concepts to the debate round. Three important criteria determine the calibre of the debate judge.

Judging Theory

A good judge must first be knowledgeable of debate theory. A standing joke in high school forensics concerns the bus drivers who judge at some tournaments, and yet debaters often complain that they would prefer those drivers to some of the so-called professionals under whom they have suffered. A teacher in the classroom or a professional in any field who was largely ignorant of the material under consideration would rapidly be ridiculed and fired; yet many who know next to nothing about debate are allowed to judge. A competent judge studies theory carefully and knows what debaters are talking about when they discuss inherency, disadvantages, or the theory of a counterplan.

The second criterion: the judge should be consistent. Just as basketball coaches ask from officials only that they "call them the same at both ends of the floor," so most debaters and their coaches are most receptive to predictable judges. A judge who changes theory on inherency from round to round or accepts justification arguments in one debate and not another will soon become the bane of fellow coaches and their debaters. If a judge's positions become well known, however, debaters will try to adapt to what the judge likes, which may, on top of everything else, make for more enjoyable rounds for the critic.

Finally, the debate should be judged on the issues and on its own merits. The judge should ignore, insofar as possible, his or her own feelings about the topic. One may hate everything that the affirmative side of the question stands for, but if the affirmative team does the better job of debating, an honest judge has to vote for them. This does not mean that aspects of the debate, such as delivery, should be ignored; obviously, if the debaters present their material in an incomprehensible manner, they can hardly be said to have done the superior job of debating. Nonetheless, if the material is understandable to the judge, the ballot should reflect the true outcome of the clash over the issues.

In addition, the judge should never debate the debaters. One may know of material which clearly wins an issue but which was not presented in the round, or one may think of a response which beats an otherwise winning argument. As ego-boosting as these brainstorms are, they should be irrelevant to the decision. The judge must decide on what the debaters did, not on what he or she knows. There are few sins that debaters hate more than the "third negative rebuttal" provided by a judge's ballot.

The only exception to the above rule is in the case of evidence falsification. Such a charge, whether made by the opposing team or originated by the judge, is extremely serious and should be pursued only in those cases where the offense seems clear. If such an act has occurred, however, the judge must then employ his own ethical standards and decide whether merely to award the issue to the other team or to forfeit the entire contest. Some levels of debate and some organizations have their own stated and rather inflexible rules concerning such unhappy occurrences.

Specifics of Judging

In addition to these general observations, a number of more specific comments need to be made concerning the role of the judge in a round. First, the judge should go into the debate prepared, having at hand enough paper, pens, etc., to perform his function. A judge who enters the room and asks the debaters to supply a flow sheet seems unprepared and rapidly loses ethos. It is also a good idea for the judge to carry a set of time cards.

The judge should flow the round as completely and carefully as possible. In some debates the speakers' presentation will make it difficult to comprehend all that has been said, and experts disagree as to what is the judge's responsibility under these circumstances. Some hold that it is incumbent upon the debater to make clear everything presented. If there is a lack of communication it is the debater's fault. Others will allow anything the debater says to be included in the decision and will ask to see reams of evidence after the debate. The most reasonable position seems to lie midway between these two extremes. Sometimes crucial words in a quotation are missed, and the judge is then doing all participants a favor by looking at the evidence. If, however, the debater simply blurbs the card at an incomprehensible rate, the judge may well be justified in refusing to aid the speaker's lack of communication. Whatever position the critic adopts on this matter should be consistently applied from round to round.

In making the decision the judge should not worry about who is winning until late in the debate; a good point at which to begin to compare issues is after the first affirmative rebuttal. At this juncture the issues which will probably be extended through the last two speeches— and which will thus have potential for being crucial— should be fairly evident. When the round ends the judge should initially look for a clear, decisive issue, such as inherency or a disadvantage, which will carry the debate negative. If none is apparent, then he must begin the more detailed search to see if the affirmative have indeed met all the requirements of a case. Generally, although certainly not always, the more quickly a decision is arrived at, the more likely it will be to go negative, since such a decision requires examination of many fewer issues than does an affirmative ballot. Generally, as well, first impressions or conclusions are the best. This is not intended to urge snap judgments, but to indicate that oftentimes the decision long agonized over will seem in retrospect less justifiable than the one made rapidly.

In preparing the ballot, the judge should always make the decision first; this is his most important duty. After that is done, the speakers should be ranked (1 through 4) and, lastly, given points. Some judges begin with the points, giving each participant what is merited on each of the available categories and then adding up the total to see who has won. This is totally wrong! Such a procedure may well miss the crucial argument which should have decided the debate. The decision should always be made first, and it should be made on the issues.

There is considerable controversy as to whether points should agree with the decision; we believe that they should. Perhaps the confusion arises from their being called "speaker points" which implies that they are somehow related to delivery. They probably should be called something less specific such as "debater points" or "rating points" which implies that they are intended to be a measure of the overall effectiveness of the individual in the round. If a debater has lost, it is difficult to claim that he is more effective than those who have beaten him.

When writing comments on the ballot— and comments should always be written— the judge should be concise and specific, telling winners why they won and the losers why they lost. Several judges have begun to carry small portable typewriters with them, thus increasing the legibility of their comments and decreasing their own writer's cramp. This is an innovation to be encouraged. Finally, avoid caustic or cruel comments on the ballot; they are neither helpful nor clever. In critiquing a round apply the Golden Rule: write as you would be written to.

Beginning judges often feel at least as uncertain in their role as do beginning debaters, and the novice critic may be very insecure indeed. Such feelings are not helped if, for example, one has to give a loss to an excellent team or is in the minority on a multi-judge panel. One must remember that such misfortunes happen even to the long-time expert and that with practice comes experience. If judges carefully do their best, confidence and competence will eventually come.

13
CHAPTER

Current Trends in Debate

All living human activities change. Indeed, failure to grow and develop is usually taken as a sign of poor health or even the death of any organism. Thus, it is not surprising that over the years debate, one of the most vital of all competitive activities, has experienced considerable change in theory and practice. The decade of the 1980's, however, saw unprecedented alteration in the manner in which inter-collegiate— and to a growing extent interscholastic— debate is carried on. This chapter will discuss in further detail current debate practice and the ways in which it differs from traditional approaches.

Like most of the practices in debate over

the decades, the current approach rests on certain theoretical concepts. Understanding the concepts is vital to a comprehension of what occurs in a debate round. Contemporary theory appears to have grown out of trends evident as early as the middle 1970's, especially the emphasis on policy making, the comparison of policy systems, and the growing tendency of judges to view themselves as arbiters of competing policies. Today's collegiate contests are almost universally viewed as jousts between rival policies, both of them different from the *status quo*. The judge is expected to decide on the basis of the argumentation in the round which side offers the superior system.

This modern approach to debate offers some striking contrasts with what was considered normal in the 1960's and the early 1970's. We will explore each of these changes in some detail. Initially, in one of the strongest contrasts, current debate has virtually abandoned the concept of presumption. Philosophical justification for this abandonment may be found in the idea of an altered world view. Presumption, it is argued, developed nearly two hundred years ago in an age whose world view— which modern science has generally proved false— differed drastically from our own. Modern debaters argue that the world is not a conservative, static place; it is, rather, a dynamic place where change is constant. Drawing on modern scientific methods and discoveries— beginning perhaps with Darwin's revolutionary concept of evolution— they maintain that the only constant in the world is change. Thus, a presumption in favor of a static *status quo* presents a false picture of what the world is really like. If change is inevitable, these theorists argue, the only question which needs to be settled in the debate is what the best change is. Therefore, presumption is assigned to history's dustbin.

Secondly, few negatives today make any concerted attack on the affirmative case (the need or advantage arguments). The reason for this is two-fold. First, with the abandoning of presumption and growing belief in the inevitability of change, traditional first negative attacks— most of which were based in some way on a defense of the *status quo*— no longer have any ground on which to rest. In addition, today's strongest negative attacks, the disadvantages, depend on the affirmative plan working; thus, few negatives wish to take the chance of weakening or contradicting their own strongest arguments. This approach of the negative does occasionally make things easier for the affirmative. For instance, the burden of inherency— which, as we remark in Chapter Seven, was long one of the most difficult the affirmative had to bear— has generally been lifted from their shoulders.

A third major alteration in the practice of debate in the 1980's was the abandonment by many negatives of several traditional forms of plan attack. Particularly, plan-meet-advantage and workability arguments have gone by the board, largely for the same reason that negatives no longer advance case attacks. They might well weaken the disadvantages on which today's debate almost totally rests. Clearly, if a

PMA prevents the plan from working, then the plan cannot operate to produce the disadvantage the negative is claiming. It would seem, from traditional theory, that this would also defeat the affirmative plan. The truth is, however, that the majority of today's policy option judges simply will not vote negative on the basis of a PMA argument no matter how strongly made; and negatives, being relatively intelligent, are willing to abandon that which will not win (PMA's) for that which will (DA's).

As the above discussion has made clear, the disadvantage now reigns as the argument without peer in modern intercollegiate debate. Simply put, negatives cannot hope to win decisions without carrying their DA's, and affirmatives are adjusting their case strategies and arguments in an attempt to weaken the DA's as much as possible. These facts of life are producing interesting aberrations in debate practice. For example, affirmatives now argue what a few years ago would have been considered a negative inherency position, maintaining that the present system will change over time to produce the same disadvantage that the negatives have claimed for the affirmative case (remember that a DA must be unique to the affirmative plan in order to win). This type of argument has led to an interesting resurgence of the counterplan (see below). In addition, affirmatives frequently reverse another traditional burden and actually try to claim for their plan as little significance as possible. The rather convoluted reasoning behind this strategy is that a very minor affirmative change can be argued to produce no real disadvantage, whereas with no presumption, even the benefit is sufficient to warrant an affirmative ballot.

As mentioned in the chapters on debating the affirmative and the negative, most affirmative teams today claim not to be defending the resolution or even the plan as an example of the resolution; rather, they maintain only that they are offering their plan as a policy option to be compared against whatever alternative the negative provides. The major reason for this position, of course, is the success of negative counter warrant arguments which present reasons for voting against the proposition as a whole, however it is interpreted by the affirmative. The result is that the proposition may well never be mentioned in the debate; it serves only to make certain that the two teams are debating more or less the same subject.

Finally, in one of the most striking changes in recent years, negatives have resuscitated the counterplan, which during the 1960's and 1970's was virtually a dead item on the college level, and have made it a major facet of modern debate practice. By rough estimate, perhaps as many as fifty percent of today's collegiate debates exhibit some form of counterplan. The re-emergence of the counterplan is rather logical given the current state of affairs. With no presumption to lose and (with the abandonment of the *status quo*) with some policy needed to weigh against the affirmative plan, the counterplan makes a good deal of sense. Most current counterplans are offered either conditionally or as exclusionary counterplans.

The most intriguing feature of many of today's counterplans, however, is the reason for which they are offered. They are not presented to defeat the affirmative by themselves; rather, they are employed to set up those all-important arguments, the disadvantages. As indicated above, affirmatives are attempting to defeat the DA's by claiming that gradual changes in the present system will produce the same problems the negatives have discovered in their plan. The negatives employ the counterplan to freeze the present system so that it cannot change and will not develop the disadvantage. This allows the negatives to claim uniqueness for their DA's and with them, hopefully, to defeat the affirmative case.

A good example of this rather complex practice may be drawn from the recent college proposition concerned with the extension of rights to citizens. Negative teams created a "give an inch, take a mile" disadvantage, arguing that any extension of civil rights would not satisfy the populace but would rather cause them to demand more and more rights until the government was rendered powerless and anarchy prevailed. Affirmatives attempted to defeat this argument by maintaining that the present system was constantly extending rights to the citizens and that if dissatisfaction prevailed under the affirmative plan, it would also be evident under the current state of affairs. Thus, negatives imposed a counterplan which froze all rights at their present levels, making any demand for further rights a unique disadvantage to the affirmative case.

This new approach to intercollegiate debate has created some interesting changes in the duties of the various speakers. With the abandonment of case attacks, first negatives now present virtually the entire negative constructive case, including technical arguments (such as topicality); a counterplan (if one is offered); and the plan objections. This, in turn, transforms the second negative constructive into a speech that is entirely refutation and extension. The negative block (2NC and 1NR) now presents a major burden for the affirmative, as the negative has the time to really develop all the outstanding arguments in complete form. Nevertheless, this arrangement probably eases the responsibility of the 1AR a bit, since that speaker now needs only to extend the responses to the plan objections rather than initiate those responses. Under the traditional system judges often sympathized with the harassed 1AR and allowed that speaker to get away with sometimes rather slipshod answers to the PO's. Now that the initial affirmative responses to disadvantages come in the 2AC, judges are holding the affirmative to more substantive replies. Finally, since both the plan objections and the answers to them must be extended twice rather than once, both the arguments and the responses to them need to be more carefully thought out than under the traditional system.

We have placed this description of current debate practice in a separate chapter to avoid the confusion inevitable if this material were included in the chapters which discuss traditional theory and practice. While we find some of the new approaches interesting— and some of them outlandish— we make no warrant either for or against this altered system of debate. We merely present this chapter as a description of what does exist, suggesting that debaters initially master the traditional approach to the activity in order to understand the changes by comparing them with past practice, and that those in charge of the activity— the coaches and judges— are the ones who have the responsibility to decide whether the new wave is more beneficial or more harmful to the activity. If the decision is for harm, it is those individuals who will have to bear the burden of change.

Index